AFRICAN FORM AND IMAGERY

DETROIT COLLECTS

With an introductory essay by Nii O. Quarcoopome

The Detroit Institute of Arts

This catalogue is published in conjunction with the exhibition "African Form and Imagery: Detroit Collects" at the Detroit Institute of Arts, June 22, 1996-January 5, 1997. The exhibition was organized by Michael Kan, curator of the Department of African, Oceanic, and New World Cultures, with co-curator Nii Quarcoopome, Assistant Professor, University of Michigan, and made possible with the support of the Friends of African and African American Art, the Founders Junior Council, the Michigan Council for Arts and Cultural Affairs, and the Detroit Institute of Arts Founders Society.

ISBN: 0-89558-145-0

Director of Publications: Julia P. Henshaw
Editor: Judith A. Ruskin
Editorial Assistant: Maria L. Santangelo
Designer: Mike Savitski, Ann Arbor, Michigan

Library of Congress
Cataloging-in-Publication Data

Detroit Institute of Arts.
    African form and imagery: Detroit collects/
        with an introductory essay by
        Nii O. Quarcoopome
            p.   cm.
    Exhibition catalog.
    Includes bibliographical references and index.
    ISBN 0-89558-145-0
    1. Art, Black—Africa, Sub-Saharan—
    Exhibitions. 2. Art—Private collections—
    Michigan—Detroit—Exhibitions. 3. Art—
    Michigan—Detroit—Exhibitions. 4. Detroit
    Institute of Arts—Exhibitions.
I. Quarcoopome, Nii O. II. Title.
N7391.65.D48 1996
709'.67'07477634—dc20   96-18754
                            CIP

CONTENTS

LENDERS TO THE EXHIBITION

Faxon Collection

Dede and Oscar Feldman

Sidney and Madeline Forbes

Charles, Gail, and Lyndsay McGee

Florence and Donald Morris

Albert Nuamah

Sophie Pearlstein

Dr. Robert E. L. Perkins

Dr. Sarah Carolyn Adams Reese

Laura and James Sherman

Joyce Marie Sims

Samuel Thomas, Jr.

and anonymous lenders

FOREWORD

THE EXHIBITION "African Form and Imagery: Detroit Collects" celebrates an important event for the Detroit community: the founding of the Department of African, Oceanic, and New World Cultures at the Detroit Institute of Arts twenty years ago. Throughout the history of the Detroit Institute of Arts great private collectors such as Robert H. Tannahill and Edsel and Eleanor Ford have formed meaningful relationships with museum directors and curators and together have created the outstanding collections of significant examples of world art visible at the museum today. "African Form and Imagery," which features over seventy fine objects from local collections along with recent major museum acquisitions, shows what is possible when museum curators reach out to collectors to develop connoisseurship and collecting activity in the community. We are extremely grateful to the Detroit collectors who have so generously lent to the show, parting with their works for more than six months so that the public can enjoy them. Our heartfelt thanks go to them all.

The Friends of African and African American Art and the Founders Junior Council, who have been our generous and constant supporters through the years, have provided sponsorship for this exhibition. The exhibition's opening will be celebrated in conjunction with Bal Africain, the Friends' annual fundraising gala event. We are particularly indebted to Sam and Rhonda Thomas, in their capacity as both leaders of the Friends and lenders to the exhibition, for their support and encouragement.

This exhibition has been greatly enriched by the participation of co-curator Nii Otokunor Quarcoopome from Ghana, who was responsible for the formatting of this exhibition and its accompanying catalogue. Following his sound advice, we have organized the exhibition according to the broad functions of objects in African life rather than in the more traditional geographical scheme. Catalogue entries were produced by a dedicated group of Quarcoopome's graduate and undergraduate students at the University of Michigan. We are particularly indebted to the following students who participated in this project: Laura Bassett Ho, Chie Tashima McKenney, Odetta Norton, Daniel Ramirez, Trevor Schoonmaker, Roberto Visani, Michelle-Lee White, with particular thanks to Pamela McKee who also worked on the label copy for the exhibition. Our special thanks also go to Professor Rowland Abiodun of Amherst College and Dr. Roy Sieber of Indiana University for their expertise and support.

Every exhibition requires the dedication and hard work of many staff members. I would particularly like to single out the exhibition's organizer, Michael Kan, curator of African Art, whose efforts in building this collection in Detroit now extend over twenty years. Louis Gauci, assisted by Robert Loew, must be commended for their imaginative use of the North Court area as a setting for the installation. Dirk Bakker's special understanding of African forms produced the magnificent photography seen in the catalogue. Judith Ruskin and Julia Henshaw were

most ably assisted by Maria Santangelo in the editing and production of the eye-catching catalogue, which was designed by Mike Savitski of Ann Arbor. Assisting with the show's organization were Pamela Watson, museum registrar, and Terry Segal, registrar for the exhibition, and Tara Robinson, exhibition coordinator. In the Conservation Services Laboratory, John Steele, Carol Forsythe, and James Leacock all provided excellent cooperation. Linda Margolin of the Education Department made valuable contributions to the programming. Special thanks must go to Lisa Roberts of the African, Oceanic, and New World Cultures Department for her outstanding contribution to the catalogue and her tireless help in writing and organizing label copy. Both David Penney and Marcia Hicks also provided essential support within the department.

We hope that "African Form and Imagery: Detroit Collects" will reach out to new viewers and create increased awareness of our outstanding permanent collection as well as of the remarkably rich resources of our community of collectors in Detroit.

Samuel Sachs II
Director

AFRICAN FORM AND IMAGERY: AN INTRODUCTION

Nii O. Quarcoopome

AFRICANS RESIDING SOUTH OF THE SAHARA live in essentially oral cultures; until a few centuries ago, when literate Islamic and European peoples made contact with these societies, few written records were kept. It is precisely because of this that Africa's visual and performing arts assume such enormous significance. A work of art may be the scroll upon which events and knowledge of the past have been inscribed. Art embodies and expresses the thoughts, lore, psychic energies, and aspirations of the peoples who produce and use it. It is the challenge for those who study African art to decode and decipher what lies embedded in its images.

The peoples of Africa have been consummate art producers since prehistoric times. Rock paintings and engravings from the deserts of the Sahara and southern Africa, dating to as early as 10,000 B.C., are among the most compelling evidence yet about past cultures. Discoveries of terracotta and metal sculptures, predominantly from West Africa, have yielded insights into how African societies interwove art and life. The Nigerian sites of Nok, Igbo Ukwu, Ife, and Benin alone represent more than two and one half millennia of art production, beginning in about 500 B.C. The significant formal and thematic continuities between past and present arts leads to the conclusion that some related practices may be just as old.

Although the art of Africa was known to the outside world for centuries, it was, ironically, European colonial intervention in the late nineteenth century that generated widespread recognition of and enthusiasm for it. As most of the old indigenous African kingdoms—Asante, Benin, Dahomey, among others—were subjugated and subsequently colonized by the European powers, large territories were opened up for economic exploitation. The continent's vast and richly diverse artistic heritage was also laid bare. Amid the ruins of royal palaces and religious shrines, once the nerve-centers of some of Africa's greatest ethnic and urban complexes, objects made in precious materials and exhibiting extraordinary technical quality emerged. These were the products of African craftspeople and, in some cases, represented more than a half millennium of uninterrupted activity.

STYLE AND ETHNICITY

From the moment of "discovery" by the West, African art's remarkable range of forms— from the astonishingly simple to the complexly dramatic—caught the attention of European artists and intellectuals. Naturally unfamiliar with the meaning and significance of their African pieces, most early collectors could only approach African art from a strictly formal perspective. Stylistic studies, therefore, became a convenient entry into a vast and largely unexplored universe of unusual shapes.

This early orientation defined the crux of African art studies up to the 1970s. William Fagg, one of its advocates, noted that the distribution of Africa's sculptural traditions coincided with ethnic and linguistic subdivisions. He saw a relationship between the tribe as a cultural entity— which he appropriately labeled "tribality"—and sculptural styles. To him, certain approaches to

> Objects are records of cultural process, and they provide unmediated access to the values and experiences of their producers—if we know how to read them.
>
> Arnold Rubin

representation are ingrained; they are part of traditions that have been passed down generation after generation. Consequently, the indigenous African artist was guided by notions of beauty and taste that were more or less shared within certain cultures. Subsequent research largely confirmed Fagg's idea of one-tribe-one-style. As such, it is now possible for us to speak of a Bamana or Yoruba or Kuba style (Fagg 1965, 1970).

However, while it is handy to view African art along these lines, the approach perpetuates the ideas that African societies are more or less hermetically sealed in so far as art production is concerned and that African artists work within the strict confines of their respective societies, lacking opportunities for innovation. Research in the last two decades has contradicted or modified both of these beliefs. Among other things, ethnic boundaries have been found to be rather porous, meaning that substantial cross-cultural artistic exchanges have occurred in the past, and continue to occur, among African peoples. Artworks themselves have moved within large geographical areas due to migrations, commerce, and a variety of other human interactions. The significance of such movements to our understanding of the history of African artistic heritage cannot be underestimated (Bravmann 1973, Kasfir 1984).

The geographical division of Africa into distinct style regions (see map, p. 6) has endured as an organizing principle in surveys of African art. In spite of its usefulness, this classification system has many inherent limitations and problems. The present international political borders imposed by Africa's European colonial masters are much too rigid and do not always coincide with ethnic boundaries. More importantly, to appreciate African visual forms for their aesthetic appeal only— as most stylistic studies do—seems too restrictive and self-serving and robs the art of its meaning, or essence. The difficulty, then, for students of African art is not so much the continent's diversity and complex visual culture, but rather the remarkable way in which art production and use intermingles with social, economic, and spiritual life.

Sub-Saharan Africa encompasses thousands of ethnic populations whose enormous cultural wealth and technological differences have long attracted the attention of anthropologists. The variety of language, belief, and social practice is astounding, but the visual arts convey certain intriguing commonalities in function. Art in Africa is viewed traditionally in a totally different light than it is in the West. In Africa, it is not viewed as an entity in itself; rather, while some objects are made to decorate, the vast majority are intended for specific purposes. African art is either utilitarian or symbolic or both. As Arnold Rubin defines it, non-Western art in general is a technology, a tool that helps humans to survive and to relate to their environment.

While sculpture and the other plastic arts have assumed a role of particular importance to Western museums and collectors, African art consists of much more. Like the arts of other non-Western cultures, such as Native American and Oceanic, those of Africa have always included products long considered crafts. Art must be more broadly construed to include architecture,

Figure **1**
Painted house in the Frafra village of Zaare, Northern Ghana.

Figure **2**
Akan appliqué textile belonging to chief Nagai Kassa VII of Agomeda Shai, Ghana.

Figure **3**
Ewe priestesses of a twin cult with painted body decorations. Agbegboza festival, Notse town, Togo.

3

household items such as baskets and ceramics, textiles, painting, and body decoration (figures 1, 2, and 3). These processes, representing a broad range of technique and medium, are often interrelated, for they share a repertoire of visual forms and motifs and, at times, function together.

In terms of utility, an African object may belong in one of the following categories: supports, containers, implements, or coverings and shelters. Symbolic uses subdivide into objects that mark or commemorate, indicate or define position, status, and power and those that perform in transactional roles, acting to mediate the relationships between humans as well as between humans and otherworldly phenomena.

FORM AND REPRESENTATION

The earlier era of unbridled generalizations about African art has given way to more substantive treatments, among them an inevitable orientation toward in-depth, cross-cultural studies. These new approaches reflect African notions about art, which differ significantly from ideas developed in the West, and have sharply focused the debate as to what constitutes art and aesthetics in Africa (Abiodun 1983). Most African cultures generally lack an equivalent for the term "art." For instance, the Gurunsi of Burkina Faso are said to use the term *bambolse*, which they define as "adorned, decorated, made more attractive," in regard to wall painting, ceramic design, and facial tatoo (van Ham and van Dijk 1980, chap. 4). This wide latitude in meaning suggests, perhaps, that we are applying the wrong criteria, or ones that are not totally attuned with the various realities of African societies.

In the African perspective, art can embody both visible and non-material aspects. The concept is hardly unique or new to African art, and has surfaced from time to time in Western art history (see Schopenhauer 1983, Arnheim 1992, Shapiro 1994), but, because art in Euro-American society is so secularized, this metaphysical dimension is often depreciated. In African art, however, the fact that there is more to the visual form than meets the eye is fundamental, and works possess an essence that gives them force. Medium plays an important role in providing artworks with efficacy because materials, too, possess innate qualities. Compositional choices, such as the type of wood employed or animal species depicted, can be intimately connected with the object's intended function.

Form, medium, and imagery are the three principal qualities through which art objects communicate. In spite of the long tradition of formal studies in African art history, the range of

4

5

possibilities regarding form has hardly been exhausted. How do Africans
compose visual forms and what factors govern the creative endeavor? In the
creation of figures, for instance, what considerations are given to anatomical
parts, subject matter, gesture, texture, color, and surface finish? There are
recurring themes in African sculpture, including mother-and-child images, riders,
hunters or warriors, strangers, and spirit images, which also contribute to similarities in form (Cole 1989). Some visual images communicate proverbs, sayings,
and oral history (figure 5).

Many other conceptual issues underlie African approaches to representation, including the contrast between humans and spirit beings which frequently
explains abstraction and naturalism; simplicity or exaggeration; as well as which
anatomical parts to single out for special attention. In many cases, the human head appears
to receive disproportionate attention, its size as much as a third of the total body length. This
emphasis may stem from a variety of beliefs relative to the head. It has been reported that the
Fang, for example, view the cranium as the sole point of access into the being and the locus of
wisdom. Consequently, the craniums of departed elders constitute emblems of group solidarity
that are imbued with spiritual powers and become the central point around which ancestral rituals
are organized (Fernandez 1982, 256-57). This may explain why so much emphasis is given to the
human head in reliquary guardian sculpture of the Fang and related peoples. Another explanation could be the widespread African belief that spirits enter and exit the human body through
the head (M. Drewal 1977, Horton 1965, Quarcoopome 1985).

In the examination of faces such as those of Ibibio white-faced and black-faced masks,
what is the distinction between spiritual and human identity? When do particular anatomical
features reflect standards of human beauty? What details of physiognomy are truly representative
of a culture's preference? What is the line between ugliness and intentional distortion? As has
been pointed out, the distorted human face lends itself to multiple interpretations; on the one
hand, as fierce or aggressive, and on the other as ugly (Sieber 1990, 343-53). Is it possible to
ground these varying elements and meanings in historical contexts to reflect changing tastes
and concepts of beauty?

MATERIALS AND ESSENCE

The most common distinctions in medium are predicated on the intrinsic value of materials,
which varies among cultures. The worth of many precious minerals, such as gold, copper, and
silver, is well accepted because of their convertibility into currency and objects of prestige. In
contrast, the value of such materials as beads and raffia may reflect entirely different principles.
Objects such as the Yoruba house of the head (*ile ori*) are frequently invested with supernormal

Figure **4**
Ceremonial stools of a chief with
coiled python and mudfish symbols. Shai, Ghana.

Figure **5**
Ewe linguist carrying a traditional
staff of office. The image depicts
the proverb: "like the cock who
is first to announce the day, it is
the chief who speaks first."
Anloga, Ghana.

spiritual energy through the inclusion of important beads. Similarly, while particular pigments and elements may appear to enrich the sculpture aesthetically, their purpose may not be exclusively decorative (figure 4). Some elements may be added for their metaphorical value such as the inclusion of raffia or bark cloth to suggest ancestral validation. Some materials are at times hardly discernible in the object, serving to counterbalance the spiritual effects of others used in the same form. Natural elements such as charcoal, seeds, fibers, bark, and resins may not be visible to the eye because they are often secreted into the object itself. Clay forming the "beard" of a Kongo minkisi may be tempered with herbs; and blood from a sacrificed animal may be smeared on a finished Dogon sculpture to make the object more efficacious (W. MacGaffey in Koloss 1990, 28-31; Ezra 1988, 48, 51).

African images are richly endowed with diverse attributes of the continent's fauna and flora (figure 2), a reflection of the artist's depth of knowledge of his or her physical environment, sense of history, and familiarity with folklore, mythology, and ritual practices. The limited number of animal species seen on objects—the leopard, pangolin, antelope, elephant, snake, bushcow, and hornbill, among others—suggests a widely shared philosophy among African cultures. The choice of a particular animal motif may be part of a prescribed formula; the number and species of birds considered suitable for a Yoruba iron diviner's staff (osanyin), for example, must adhere to established standards. As the most important emblem in the distinctive ritual paraphernalia of a diviner, the staff must not only be manufactured from forged iron but also include in its iconography a hierarchical arrangement of single or multiple birds. The power of the diviner to fulfill his spiritual responsibilities to protect society resides within this complex imagery. Whether the bird is rendered naturalistically or not is immaterial. The number of birds on the staff equals its potency (Thompson 1983, 45). The imagery is deemed suitable because it embodies a truth or an essence that helps the object fulfill its desired purpose.

Animal representations can express different shades of meanings. Some creatures are selected because of their perceived magical potential, some for their physical prowess, and still others for their unique attributes. Feathered headdresses, for instance, identify some Kongo minkisi figures with forces of the sky, such as storms and birds of prey. The inclusion of red parrot feathers in particular endow the figures with the capacity to communicate secrets (W. MacGaffey in Koloss 1990, 30). While animal motifs can serve as visual metaphors, in some cases, the intent seems to be to exploit a creature's full spiritual potential through the inclusion of actual body parts (figure 6). Selective use of particular birds' feathers, animal teeth, furs, skins, bones, or horns, as is common in minkisi sculpture from Central Africa, may be part of an approach designed to either enrich the visual vocabulary or to transfer the spiritual power of an animal to the object (Ben-Amos 1984, Roberts and Roberts 1995). Both qualities insure the object's capacity to function in a specific way.

6

THE FORCE OF ART

Masks and figures essentially function in one or more of the following capacities: to depict humans; to intercede in or mediate human relations with spirits; to impersonate or personify spirits, making the invisible visible (Roy 1987, 40); to validate norms; to control society; to impart knowledge; and, in the case of masquerades, to transform their wearers.

The philosophy of an in-dwelling potential of art objects abounds among African peoples (Firth 1973). For example, in Yoruba thought, every element of creation possesses its own vital force known as *ase*, which provides it with a life of its own, assures its individuality, and enables it to affect others. This concept is extended to art objects, as well (see H. Drewal et al. 1989). The Dogon of Mali call such a force *nyama*, a naturally existing vitality in all things that can be augmented with sacrifice (Ezra 1988, 48, 51). The Dangme and Ewe peoples of southeastern Ghana describe the related concepts of *hewam* and *ama* (Quarcoopome 1993a, 1993b). The Dan people of Liberia espouse beliefs about a phenomenon known as *du*, which has been described as "an essential force" that resides in masks and insures that vitality (Fischer and Himmelherber 1984, 6-8). For many religious works, the force contained in them is as crucial as the visual form. Central African *minkisi* sculpture is viewed more as a container for potent medicines than as an art object. Indeed, the spirit force in a *nkisi* figure is so vital that the *nganga,* or ritual specialist, responsible for the medicine is given full credit for the work of art, minimizing the contribution of the sculptor (Hersak in Koloss 1990, 62).

When the African artist follows the prescribed formula, his creation acquires a certain vitality that gives it identity or character. For most religious and magical figures, this spiritual investment constitutes an irreducible core. This non-visible dimension or essence could surely rate alongside certain formal innovations as a significant contribution of sub-Saharan African cultures.

The Westerner accustomed to experiencing art mostly within the ascetic museum environment may dismiss these notions as an attempt to further mystify an art that is already considered enigmatic because of our own inadequate knowledge. Our inability to comprehend the purpose of African art and to discern its real social meaning stems in part from our lack of opportunity to experience art in the same way an African creator or user does. When seen in its proper cultural context, the mask or figure may operate in consonance with other objects; or it may act as a visual counterpart to a specific incantation or spell that may only be vocalized during a performance; or it may appear before a special audience. Its essence may also exist only in harmony with the essences of related forms.

Denis Williams (1974), in his much-acclaimed volume entitled *Icon and Image*, makes what may well be the most profound observation about religion in Africa. Basing his study on

Figure **6**
Chief's headgear decorated with skin and leather-encased charms. Treasury of Nene Nagai Kassa VII. Agomeda-Shai, Ghana.

Yoruba culture, he notes the belief that certain objects of art are bonded with archetypal material buried in shrines. The subterranean material, which often consists of animal, plant, and other natural substances, is what anchors spiritual energy or force in the art object. A sculpture would, therefore, need to be brought into physical contact with its base within the shrine in order to be effective. The image is only a focus of worship, and its perceived capacity to act in a specific, predictable fashion is neutralized once it is detached from its underpinning.

Research among the Ga and Dangme of southern Ghana reveals a similar dynamic relationship between the object and its shrine base. Even more interesting is the emerging discourse on secret knowledge in Africa which suggests that some objects function only in connection with spells and incantations verbalized within particular performances (Quarcoopome 1993). These findings raise vital questions regarding the total significance of certain so-called "power figures" from Africa found in American and European museums. Can we accurately refer to a shrine piece uprooted from its African environment as a power object when it is separated from its essence? Are such art objects without these spiritual associations considered art to the African mind?

CONTEXT

Social context is of crucial importance in any interpretive study, for rituals and other ceremonies provide the settings within which most African works of art are displayed and used. Musical accompaniment, verbal references, dance gestures, and costume are all crucial elements that complement and enhance the functions of the work of art (figures 7 and 8). In fact, *du* forces, for whom most Dan masks are carved, are said to prefer to manifest themselves in dramatic settings (Fischer and Himmelherber 1984, 6-8). To be fully appreciated, art must be observed, therefore, in situ. While a substantial amount of African art is created of perishable materials, and many pieces are less than a century old, we can assume on the basis of the depth of the traditions from which they have sprung that they represent recent interpretations of much older forms.

A ritual practice, masquerade performance, or prayer ceremony can be viewed as more than just a means to situate art within a particular social milieu; they also integrate the past into daily life. In the same vein, the re-enactment of myth, of the actions of a cultural hero, and of the lives lived by human ancestors embody a sense of history. Prayers, songs, liturgies and dances performed both privately and publicly forge a bond with the past in ways that are both experiential and didactic. The significance of many important presentations featuring works of art—for example, the Bamana *chi wara*, Yoruba *egungun*, and Kuba royal masking—hinges on the ability of those performances to reflect and to recapitulate a critical aspect of social existence: the pursuit of life must be validated by the non-living. In acknowledgment and celebration of

7

the dead and the past, a society regains its energy to continue living.
Such cycles are at the core of African ideas about time. While the
notion of time may be expressed linearly in terms of a past, present,
and future, the cycle of life, death, and reincarnation seems to be
very pervasive. By considering this African philosophy, the writing
of African art history may become a less daunting task, for much
of the continent's art is part of living traditions, beliefs, and practices
that are relived periodically. African art is neither static nor final.
Indeed, its dynamism has been noted, perhaps no more poignantly
than by scholar Herbert Cole, who wrote in regard to Ibo *mbari* art:
"mbari has always evolved to take on the preoccupations of time and space." It comprises
"fragments of the past tumbled together surreally with reflections of the present and hopes
of the future" (Cole 1988, 54).

Figure **7**
War chief in regalia decorated
with magic charms and bearing
fly whisks of lion and elephant
tails. Old Ningo town, Ghana.

Figure **8**
Alaga masquerade performing
cleansing rites during
Agbogboza festival. Notse,
Togo, 1988.

ARTISTS AND PATRONS

Few African "traditional" practitioners in the field of visual art have ever been known
by name, even though various empirical studies show that accomplished artists were widely
acknowledged and appreciated both inside and outside their communities (Ross 1984; Abiodun
in Drewal et al. 1994). Conceptually, a culture's shared ideals and aspirations will always be
manifested in its arts, but the unique creative abilities of artists also deserve to be recognized.
Frequently disregarded is the great latitude enjoyed by traditional African artists, which allows
them to be innovative in their creations and express personal feelings even though they are
working under strictures that often dictate various elements. Most artists work in the shadows
of their masters, having acquired their skill over a lengthy apprenticeship (figure 9). At least a
modest self-awareness is ingrained in every African artist and emerges in his or her particular
approaches to visual form, finishing, and imagery. The Asante comb's particular linear cross-
hatched motif, for example, appears on other strikingly similar pieces probably made by the
same hand (see Antiri 1974) and is perhaps the artist's attempt to leave his mark. Many such
artists' signatures may remain undetected, however, as long as so little information is known
about their creators.

Most African artists appear to be anonymous not by choice but because their individual
identities generally become subsumed within their ethnic identities. Also, the very notion of the
artist as a single individual may be deceptive in cases where more than one specialist is responsible for the work. The manufacture of a Yoruba *egungun*, for example, combines the efforts of a
sculptor, who makes the mask headdress, and a tailor, who sews the elaborate attached costume

8

(Wolff 1982, 67). Typically, however, the artist represents a unique breed with a multiplicity of talents—a diviner, a musician, a poet, a healer, and a magician. He or she is able to translate a people's imagination and thoughts into visual reality, a poet who skillfully encapsulates in visual forms the verbal wisdom of his group. In sum, he or she is a person of prodigious knowledge.

AFRICAN FORM AND IMAGERY: DETROIT COLLECTS

The collecting frenzy that followed Africa's debut into the world art market at the turn of the twentieth century has yet to abate. Originally viewed as curios or exotica, African pieces have now been elevated to their rightful places among the ranks of the world's finest cultural achievements. Western museums, auction houses, and collectors have contributed immensely to this achievement by playing a dual and often contradictory role. On the one hand, through their enthusiastic acquisition of African objects, these institutions have made the creativity of African art accessible to a larger viewing public. On the other hand, such institutions have inadvertently influenced our perception of what constitutes art by what they collect and exhibit.

In attempting to make sense of a very diverse and largely unknown corpus of work, this exhibition and volume have three objectives: to seek a deeper understanding of each piece in terms of its function, meaning, context, and significance; to gain cross-cultural perspectives on the production and uses of art in African societies; and last, to widen the scope of knowledge about African works of art and thereby contribute to the scholarship in the field.

The objects presented have been divided into four categories. "For Spirits and Ancestors" addresses art created to honor, communicate with, or signify the presence or power of otherworldly phenomena. These pieces include depictions of mythic, legendary, and historical personages, deities, and a variety of forces that influence life and survival. "To Protect and Defend" explores a broad range of forms, ranging from divination and healing devices to weaponry, which were designed to aid in counteracting negative human and spiritual forces, such as witchcraft and bad magic. "Symbols of Passage" reflects on the vast group of objects that African peoples use to commemorate, facilitate, or record transitions in life, mainly birth, puberty, marriage, death, and the afterlife. "Power and Display" explores the symbols that help to differentiate roles, positions, and material well-being among people.

This breakdown is neither all-encompassing nor always clear-cut, since some pieces may serve more than one function. For instance, there are objects that are clearly utilitarian as containers—such as the Kuba, Luba, and Chokwe vessels—but which may equally be invested with the symbolism of personal philosophy, wealth, and prestige. While more and more field

9

Figure **9**
Asanta carver at work.
Kumasi, Ghana, 1995.

data is being collected, making it easier to discuss the function, meaning, and significance of certain major works, the stark reality is that such detailed information such as where, how, and when a particular work of art was produced and the precise context of its use are often not available for many pieces. The ability to explore the objects in their totality is thus severely curtailed, as illustrated in this catalogue by the uneven discussion of individual works.

Although much has been accomplished in African art scholarship in the last half century, the discipline still lacks relevant information about most African art producers for several reasons. First, the focus of research continues to be too narrow, dwelling on a relatively limited number of cultures. And, because of the strong interest in the plastic arts, there exists a significant imbalance in scholarship. Second, most specialists lack the requisite proficiency in the languages of the people they study even though it is now all too clear that such competence can significantly enhance understanding of the arts. And last, there is little collaboration within the discipline, let alone across disciplines. In view of these factors, not even three decades of active research and publication can boast complete comprehension of Africa's artistic heritage. Yet, through resolve, the scholarship has inched closer to the ideal of achieving greater understanding of Africa's visual arts with each successful exploration through public exhibitions and insightful catalogues. Like many that have preceded it, this catalogue does not boast a grand solution to the existing problems facing African art studies; in fact, it may end up raising even more issues. That, too, is healthy.

FOR SPIRITS AND ANCESTORS

BELIEFS ABOUT THE SPIRIT WORLD have long been the primary source of most African imagery. Indeed, cosmological ideas have informed most interpretations of African visual art, from the fabled antique rock art of the late stone age to more recent innovations. As long as religion plays a crucial role in the daily life of Africans, concerns about relationships between humans and spirits will continue to dominate the arts. Religious images—visual forms that represent, signify, or impersonate otherworldly beings and forces—constitute a problematic and elusive category in African art. Although there have been some excellent explorations of the subject (Siroto 1976), the issue of precisely what factors influence representation and imagery poses challenges to historical investigation. Indeed the identity of certain so-called ancestor figures is now being questioned. The term ancestor is used with caution, for in some cases it is inaccurate and may merely serve as a convenience for pieces that lack more detailed information (Siroto 1976; 20, 22-24).

Three classes of spirits receive special attention in African artistic representation. First, there are the divinities or nature deities said to reside in natural phenomena such as lightning, rivers, and the sea. These principalities are, by virtue of their extreme capriciousness, considered to be deserving of constant propitiation to insure their good will toward humans. Second are the ancestral spirits—souls of distant and recently departed members of society—who are believed to possess the ability to influence life and survival. They enforce traditional norms and intercede on behalf of the living in times of crisis. Last is the earth spirit. While most African cultures believe in the presence of these spirits, they differ in their degrees of emphasis on any one or more of these categories.

Artistic depictions, too, reveal some variety in the ways in which these imaginary beings are given concrete visual form. Masks and figures are the most common, but where a spirit cannot be conceived in sculptural terms, it may be recognized in textiles or venerated through diverse performances. Spirit beings have identities which may be conveyed by accentuating their key attributes. Orally transmitted verses, songs, and prayers are a principal source of information about deities, as illustrated in the case of the Yoruba trickster deity, Eshu, whose distinctive visual characteristics—the phallic protuberance emanating from the back of the skull, the flute, the bulging forehead, and the multiple gender references—are alluded to in Yoruba oral literature (Bascom 1973, Drewal et al. 1989). But such depictions of African divinities are a rarity. Frequently, a representation may be cryptic and metaphorical, often emphasizing only motifs associated with the deity's cult or emblems carried by its devotees, as in the case of the double-axed dance wand of Shango, the thunder god.

The most pervasive African practice uses a sculpted image as both a temporary abode for the godly spirit and a focus of worship. In most cases, the size of such a religious icon has no bearing on either the power contained in it or the god's relative importance in the pantheon.

Indeed some of the most spiritually powerful images are the least imposing. The miniature Songye figure would seem to support this assertion. Even more importantly, because many African deities are never actually depicted, some sacred images likely represent devotees of gods, as in the case of the pair of Yoruba Shango pieces. For such objects, one is confronted with the problem of determining their precise significance.

Many art objects are considered surrogates of the dead, symbolizing the continued presence of departed souls. Some objects, too, function as guardians of the dead, for a fitting burial may not be entirely adequate. The mortal remains, especially skeletal parts of an important family or village elder may be buried and then subsequently recovered for preservation. Because the remains are portable, the living can travel with them. Visual forms may be created solely to signal the presence of such sacred relics or to guard against their desecration. Fang reliquary heads from Cameroon and Gabon perform such a protective function. They are also imbued with immense religious significance because, besides depicting the ancestors, they are said to be capable of interceding on behalf of humans. The collection of craniums which these sculptures are intended to protect promotes a sense of corporate solidarity with the dead, becoming the "sacra around which [ancestral] rituals are organized." Like reliquary images, anthropomorphic harps in Fang culture may also serve as vehicles of communication between the living and the dead (Fernandez 1982, 256, 416).

Nonetheless, relics aside, artistic forms created to serve commemorative purposes consti-tute a significant portion of African sculpture. The shrines into which they are incorporated vary in size and may be either public or private depending on the sociopolitical position of the deceased. Memorial figures are frequently commissioned for those individuals who have contributed in various ways to the community or have simply led exemplary lives. An ancestral shrine normally includes a central figure, animal or human, that acts either as a receptacle for the soul of the deceased or as a point of contact with his or her spirit. Such an image embodies visual elements reflecting the kinship, cult, or political affiliation of the ancestor. Pieces intended to venerate historical personages reflect social status and kinship affiliation through the use of prestige symbols and totemic motifs. In general, sculptures said to represent ancestors frequently portray idealized anatomical features, elaborate adornment, emblems of secular authority, and gestures that project moral uprightness.

The artistic depiction of ancestors takes two forms. There is a unique class of mythic or legendary personages who are connected to societal origins. In some cultures, the identities of cultural heroes seem fairly established. For example, the Kuba royal Mwaash a Mbooy mask is said to depict the founder of the present dynasty, King Shyaam. Countless variations of the Bamana mythical antelope, *Chi Wara,* exists in the art of the Bamana and related peoples of Mali. Chi Wara is said to be the cultural hero who taught the Bamana how to farm. There are

Royal ancestor shrine, Benin
kingdom, Nigeria: Altars to
Ovonramwen (background)
and Eweka II (front).

other representations, however, for which attributions are far less certain, such as the so-called *nommo* images of the Dogon also from Mali (Ezra 1988).

A second category of sculpture consists principally of depictions of historical personages whose kinship ties can still be traced in contemporary societies. Such memorial figures constitute by far the great majority of ancestral art. The more generic the sculptural depiction, the more distant is the relationship to the living and the less specificity there is in terms of his or her historical or human identity. Human and animal figures created to commemorate political leaders are often found in the context of elaborate public or private altars dedicated to those individuals. However, not all objects destined for the ancestral altar may be given specific human identities. Conventionally, Benin royal terracotta heads, assigned to the early period of the kingdom (ca.1450-1550), were presumably reserved for brasscasters while their cast bronze and wooden counterparts remained a prerogative of royalty and provincial chiefs, respectively.

Some spirits do not possess identities of their own, so the forms given them, whether human or animal, may be intended for purposes other than identification. For example, in the cases of the Atyie or Ebrie spirit spouse figure from Côte d'Ivoire and the Bundu *sowo* mask of the Mende of Sierra Leone, idealized human features are employed to allure and appease the spirits and ensure their good-will.

The belief that certain art objects can literally act independently of human use by virtue of their own innate powers is particularly strong in some African cultures. For the Dan of Liberia, the ceremonial carved wooden rice ladle is said to act on its own to facilitate the work of the *wunkirle*, the most generous woman, who caters to visitors to her community. Such objects are invested with spiritual properties that lend themselves to manipulation by persons with the requisite knowledge. These images embody magical essences that increase or decrease with the level and frequency of the object's use. The residing forces remain indestructible throughout the life span of the art work.

African spirit images carved of wood are perishable, and when important religious icons deteriorate, they may be replaced with substitutes and their potent forces transferred to the newly made piece through prescribed ritual. The object's inherent force is periodically activated with song, rhythmic accompaniment, or incantations, with each occurence testing and sharpening the effectiveness of the power inside.   NQ

HEAD

Benin, Nigeria

Terracotta

25.4 x 15.2 cm

(10 x 6 in.)

Faxon Collection

In the Kingdom of Benin in southeastern Nigeria, the placement of commemorative heads on ancestral altars is an ancient custom, reportedly dating back to the first dynasty of the Ogiso or "Rulers of the Sky" before the fourteenth century (Ben-Amos 1980, 14-15). The practice reflects the Edo peoples' view of the head as symbolizing "life and behavior in this world, [and] the capacity to organize one's actions in such a way as to survive and to prosper" (Bradbury 1973, 263, quoted in Ben-Amos 1980, 46-50). Nowhere is this more apparent than on the ancestral altars of the divine kings, or *obas,* whose survival and prosperity are perceived as one with the welfare of the kingdom.

For several centuries, royal commemorative heads have been created of cast brass, while those of chiefs are carved from wood. Today, terracotta heads like this example are reserved for the members of the brasscasters' guild, although tradition states that they also adorned the royal altars of the Ogiso. In addition, they were reputedly found on shrines in the city's quarter reserved for the "sons of the soil," original owners of the land, as well as that for the guild responsible for spiritually cleansing the kingdom following the violation of taboos (Ben-Amos 1980, 15). The difference in materials for the later kings, chiefs, and casters is significant, since the indestructibility of brass suggests the permanence of the royal line and thus serves as an eternal reminder of the past king's accomplishments (Ben-Amos 1991, 38). This is but one example of the rigidly demarcated status differences pervasive in traditional Edo society, where the ownership of brass was a royal prerogative.

Until the British sacking of the capital in 1897, the brasscasters, like many other specialized artisans, worked solely for the oba. In addition to the impressive brass commemorative heads, they produced memorial tableaux, full figures, plaques, and small hip masks. The importance of these objects in the ritual life of the kingdom ensured the casters a privileged position at court, where they were granted titles in recognition of their service.

The origins of brasscasting in Benin are obscure, but are commonly linked in oral tradition with the beginnings of the current dynasty around 1300 A.D. The fifth oba, Oguola, is said to have sent to the Yoruba city of Ife for a brasscaster to make the ritual objects which until then had been sent from that city (Egharevba 1960, 12, cited in Ezra 1992, 11). Igueghae, this early Yoruba caster, is thus regarded as the founder of the guild, and his descendants make a sacrifice to him annually at a shrine containing terracotta heads reputedly brought from Ife as models (Duchâteau 1994, 37).

The belief in an Ife origin for the commemorative heads has been used to formulate a chronology for the production of brass heads, with the most naturalistic examples—those closest in style to the bronze heads of Ife—viewed as the earliest. Most terracotta heads, like this one, are fairly realistic in their facial treatment, supporting an early date, yet thermoluminescent testing of some such heads has revealed a longer period of production than has been postulated for the early brasses (Ezra 1992, 48). Moreover, it has been suggested that the early brass heads are not royal ancestral heads at all, but rather represent the heads of those enemies captured in war and may have also been produced for a much longer period of time than is generally thought (Ben-Amos 1980, fig. 16).

This, like many of the terracotta heads, features a large hole at the top of the skull. One of the brasscasting chiefs has stated that these would have allowed for the insertion of an ivory tusk when the terracotta heads were used on the altars of the Ogiso rulers (Ben-Amos 1980, fig. 12). However, the fragility of terracotta makes this seem unlikely, as the heavy weight of a tusk would surely damage the heads. It seems more plausible that a carved wooden attachment may have been used in the past, particularly since ivory has long been a high-status material reserved for the obas.

The treatment of the hair on this piece as a series of small, incised lines arranged in horizontal rows is similar to that on the early brass heads, as is the tight-fitting collar suggesting strands of beads. The hair style depicts a type of plaiting known from early-twentieth-century photographs of the neighboring Ibo people, and was probably also worn by the Edo in the past (Kathy Curnow, personal communication, 1996). The raised marks above each eye represent scarification patterns. Three are generally used for Edo men, four are used for Edo women and foreigners (Ezra 1992, 33). The stains on the face were likely caused by the pouring of libations during commemorative rites.   PM

Provenance: Roger de la Burde, France

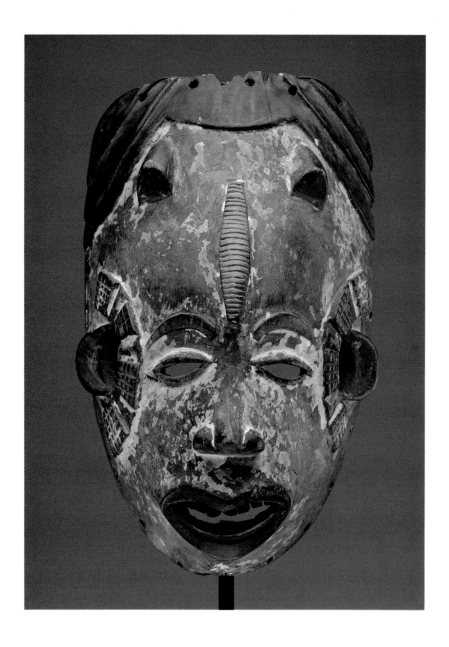

2. MAIDEN SPIRIT MASK

Igbo (Ibo), Nigeria
Wood, pigment
25.4 x 15.2 cm
(10 x 6 in.)
The Collection of
Sophie Pearlstein

The tremendous variation of mask styles found amongst the Igbo of southeastern Nigeria attests both to the cultural and historical heterogeneity of the region and to the importance of masquerade in the social and religious life of the people. Igbo mask types are hierarchically arranged, from the least important ones owned and danced by the youngest groups, to the most powerful which are reserved for senior titled men. All are viewed as incarnations of spirits and command respect, particularly from the uninitiated. Masks are owned individually or collectively by age-grades, secret societies, or villages, but with very few exceptions they are danced by men (Cole and Aniakor 1984, 111-13).

Broadly speaking, Igbo masks may be perceived as either beautiful or "heavy" and threatening (Cole and Aniakor 1984,

113). Of the former, probably the most common type is the "maiden spirit" mask or *Agbogho mmanwu*. Worn by men between the ages of thirty and fifty, "maiden spirit" masks are more spiritually significant than are the masks worn by their younger brothers. Like most Igbo masks, the maiden spirits are perceived as the "incarnate dead" but are never considered portraits of specific deceased individuals. Instead, they are believed to embody important attributes of feminine grace and beauty, and while clearly entertaining, also suggest the ancestors' continuing interest in the fertility of the land and the people (Cole and Aniakor 1984, 120).

Although maiden spirit masks show tremendous stylistic variation, they all share certain features that relate to the Igbo aesthetics of female beauty. First of these is their pale (usually white) surface, which is an exaggeration of the light skin tone that is considered ideal. A pale complexion may be preferred because it allows for a bold

contrast with the beautiful painted designs which are an ancient form of cosmetic adornment. Moreover, white is associated with the spirit realm and also suggests moral purity (Cole and Aniakor 1984, 121).

Fine facial features, including a straight narrow nose and small mouth, are preferred. Facial tattoos are often strategically placed to draw attention to these delicate features. The mask's surfaces are usually smooth and shiny in imitation of well-tended, beautiful skin. The masquerade costume is tight-fitting and brightly colored, drawing attention to the full pointed breasts and slim waistlines which are considered hallmarks of a young woman's figure. Although the dances progress from very slow, almost coquettish movements to highly athletic performances, the masqueraders must carry themselves in an upright and dignified manner, reflecting the morally pure stature of these idealized maidens (Cole and Aniakor 1984, 121).

Maiden spirit masquerades are most commonly performed at the "Fame of the Maidens" or *Ude Agbogho* festival which was formerly held each year in certain regions. Although the masqueraders are male, the site is cleared and prepared by young women, who sing songs of praise for both real and spiritual maidens (Cole and Aniakor 1984, 120-21). While the audience is aroused by a lively musical performance, the masqueraders enter the area, led by a man carrying a female image known as "Eagle seeks out beauty" (Cole and Aniakor 1984, 124).

Several maiden spirits arrive together, including a "mother" and her "daughters." The former, characterized by a slower, more dignified bearing and dance style, is evocative of the power and grace of senior titled women. While her mask resembles those of her "daughters," her costume, featuring flatter breasts, refers to her having borne children. While the "mother" watches, the "maidens" begin their dances of slow, shy steps. As the performance continues, the dancers quicken, in increasingly athletic displays of prowess, culminating with a circular dance by the "maidens," after which they retire from the clearing (Cole and Aniakor 1984, 124-25).

The "maiden spirit" masquerades pay tribute to the ancestors whose beneficence insures the fertility of humans and the land. In this regard, it is significant that they may also appear at the funerals of highly respected women, serving as spirit guides to the realm of the ancestors (Cole and Aniakor 1984, 128).   RV

Provenance: Daniel Indelli, New York

❸ FEMALE FIGURE

Ebrie or Atyie,
Côte d'Ivoire
Wood
h. 28.6 cm (11 ¼ in.)
Anonymous Loan

❹ FEMALE FIGURE

Bete, Côte d'Ivoire
Wood
h. 58.4 cm (23 in.)
Faxon Collection

In eastern Côte d'Ivoire, a cluster of ethnic groups referred to as the Lagoon peoples make and use wooden statues in healing and divination. These figures are often thought of as portraits, either of diviners or of guardian spirits, and may be named after the individuals with whom they are identified. They do not, however, necessarily share any physical resemblance to their owners. Instead, they reflect societal ideals of feminine or masculine beauty (Visona 1990, 57).

Documentation about these figures is scant, as is information on much of the art from this region. Due to the lack of suitable landings and trading posts in the area, Europeans did not establish contacts with people from this area until the mid-nineteenth century (Visona 1990, 54). This explains the scarcity of written evidence on the area. The Lagoon peoples may share a distant ethnic origin with the Akan in Ghana. The Bete in contrast live in southwestern Côte d'Ivorie.

Divination statues such these are often referred to as "people of wood" or "children of wood" (Visona 1984, 93) and act as intermediaries between the human world (that of the diviner) and the spirit world. Most diviners among the Lagoon peoples are women, and therefore most statues depict female figures. A diviner generally has one statue, through which she relays messages to the spirit world. Likewise, the statue may contact a diviner with important information through a dream. The figures are also believed to hold powerful forces that can assist or harm the owner. Because of their human form, figural statues rather than non-representational objects are considered much more useful as links with the spirit world (Visona 1984, 105).

Diviners among the Baule and Lagoon peoples commission works that represent a type of beauty recognized as ideal, so as to appeal to both humans and spirits. The bulbous legs, for example, refer to well-developed calf muscles, considered attractive among the Baule (Ravenhill 1994, 30). The sculptures generally have scarification, even though the practice of human ornamentation stopped in the early twentieth century. Like the Baule, the Atye scarification represents beauty and also individualizes a statue. Added beads

and cloth serve the same purpose. The hairstyles are often composed of ridged hemispherical shapes, representing hairstyles worn by Akye women at the beginning of this century. For these figures to become divining tools, they must be rubbed with kaolin and annointed with oils as they are activated by their owners (Visona 1984, 99).

The Lagoon forms bear a striking similarity to others made by the nearby Baule who call them "Other World mates" (Ravenhill 1994, 26). "Spirit mates" have also been documented among some Lagoon peoples (Visona 1990, 60). If the Other World spirit contacts his or her earth mate demanding recognition and attention (usually by creating difficulties in the person's marriage or childbirth), a diviner may recommend that a carving of the spirit be made. This enables the person to maintain an on-going relationship with the spirit. One contacts his or her spirit through dreams and makes small offerings to the carved representation. Problems between earth and spirit mates can then be averted or resolved.

Both standing female figures are clearly examples from this tradition. The second piece may be Bete (an ethnic group near the Lagoon peoples), based on the protruding forehead, conical breasts, geometric scarification pattern, and, particularly, the angled joining of the legs to the torso (see Phillips 1995, fig. 5.131). Precise identification is difficult, however, because of the wide movement of these types of figures and figural styles throughout Côte d'Ivoire and southwestern Ghana.

In recent times, these statues have been carved for purposes other than divination. For example, a dancer may have her portrait commissioned and carry it as an indication of her own beauty as well as her dancing abilities. Statues may also be carved to commemorate deceased twins or sets of twins (Visona 1990, 58-59). Nonetheless, although their use has dwindled, divination seems to be the most consistent purpose for such figures.   LBH

Provenance:
3. Philip Sanfield, Detroit, Michigan
4. Pace Gallery, New York

⑤ PAIR OF SHANGO FIGURES

Yoruba, Nigeria

Wood

h. 57.2 cm (22¹/₂ in.)

Faxon Collection

Shango worship is among the most widespread spiritual practices of the Yoruba. The story of Shango's origin and evolution to an *orisha*, or god, as well as the rituals and art forms associated with the deity vary considerably from area to area and are frequently individualized by worshippers. Traditionally, the Yoruba of Nigeria believe that Shango, the fourth king of the ancient Yoruba kingdom Oyo-Ile, was deified after death. This occurred after his tyrannical reign which had resulted in his subjects' rejection of him, ultimately leading to his suicide. The powerful thunderstorm that followed Shango's violent death ravaged the city, causing extensive loss of life and property. While a Yoruba thunder deity may have existed prior to Shango's rule, he is now the historical figure who has come to be identified with the force of thunder and lightning.

Shango mythology and worship reveal fundamental Yoruba social and moral concerns about violence, abuse of power, disgrace, submission, and fear. When a devotee is possessed by Shango, he or she is said to cross the boundary of rational and conventional behavior, giving voice to the latent violence within the being. Persons who risk this kind of spiritual experience become mediators who articulate the troubling ambiguities that generally characterize relations with the spirit world (Fagg 1982, 75).

Shango priests and priestesses serve as mediators between the material and spiritual realms. As mediums, they bring the orisha's spirit into the physical presence of others. Preparation for their role includes the implantation of a ball of medicine beneath the skin on the crown of the head. It is this medicine which is believed to attract the spirit of Shango into the body of the priest or priestess. Yoruba artworks often portray priests and devotees with swollen heads, suggesting the presence of the god within the head.

These two figures depict a male and a female devotee who hold several important emblems associated with Shango worship. In his right hand, the male figure carries an *oshe shango* or dance staff with its typical double axe motif. Legend says that these Late Stone Age axes create sparks when they are hurled to Earth by Shango to punish his enemies. Although one of the celts has broken off of this example, the doubling of the motif refers to Shango's role as the protector of twins (Drewal, Pemberton, and Abiodun 1989, fig. 176). A *laba shango* is draped over the male figure's left shoulder. These leather bags are used by priests to collect the magical celts from sites where lightning has struck.

The female figure holds a gourd rattle in her right hand. These are used in the dance and performance which initiate possession trance. Over her left shoulder, she wears a cowry vestment often worn by priests to indicate their importance and status in society. Because cowries are an ancient form of currency, they also suggest the wealth that was Shango's in life and which he can bestow upon those who follow him.   RV

Provenance: David Ackley, Ann Arbor, Michigan

6 STANDING FIGURE

Baga, Guinea
Wood
h. 57.2 cm (22¹/₂ in.)
Anonymous Loan

Despite the popularity of Baga sculpture among Western collectors, very little is known about this small Guinean ethnic group. The Baga are related linguistically and culturally to the Temne of Sierra Leone, and both groups migrated south from the Futa Djallon highlands beginning in the fourteenth century. Successive groups moved south until the eighteenth century, and the Baga now live in small clusters among various groups on the Atlantic coast. Periodic invasions by the Nalu, Susu, Maninka, Fulbe, and others succeeded in separating the Baga from the Temne, and in many instances these conquering groups subsumed the Baga both culturally and linguistically. In modern times, the conversion to Islam and the transition to nationalism have essentially destroyed what remained of traditional Baga culture (Lamp 1986, 64).

This cultural and linguistic deterioration has profoundly affected interpretations of Baga arts. As Frederick Lamp has noted, the brief fieldwork carried out on the Baga has usually employed the Susu language. This has therefore necessitated reliance on foreign terms for the description of ritual and has generated essentially Susu interpretations of Baga religious and social constructs. The most notable error, and one that has been widely repeated in the literature, is the ascription of the so-called *Simo* society to these peoples. According to Lamp's informants, Simo is the Susu term for anything sacred, and the Baga have not ever had such a society (Lamp 1986, 65).

These same linguistic problems have plagued interpretations of the famous *Nimba* headdresses that so closely resemble this standing figure. In Baga, the large female-figured masks are termed *Dämba* or *Dämba-ko-Pön,* and are neither owned by the initiation societies nor even connected with initiation as has been asserted. Rather,

they are the property of villages, where they were apparently associated more with women than with men. Lamp's Baga informants noted that Dämba is not a goddess at all, nor even a spirit, although her male dancer was perceived as a spirit while performing (Lamp 1986, 65).

Because of the very close formal similarities between this standing figure and the Dämba masks, it seems probable that they share symbolic associations. While mistakenly labeled as a "goddess of fecundity," these female images are instead suggestive only of a woman who has borne children, as attested by the fallen breasts that are usually depicted. It is true, however, that usage of Dämba was linked with concerns for both agricultural and human fertility and growth (Lamp 1986, 66). The standing figures were reputedly carved in male/female pairs and placed between the village and the forest in small thatched huts. There they both protected the village and helped to ensure fertility (van Geertruyen 1976, 115).

Unfortunately, the iconographical elements of both the standing figures and the Dämba masks have not been addressed in the literature. The curious pose of this example, with chin resting on upstretched hands, is identical to that of a very similar figure in the Stanley Collection in Iowa (Roy 1992, fig. 24). Whether it should be regarded as contemplative or prayerful is unclear. Interpretations of the hair style, with its pronounced sagital crest surrounded by incised indications of plaiting, typical of Dämba masks as well, are also unrecorded. Both the shape of the nose and head are reminiscent of the sculptural styles of the Sudanic regions to the east, as are the abstracted C-shaped ears, and may be a retention from the Baga's geographic heritage in the Futa Djallon highlands. However, the fully rounded treatment of the body finds clearer parallels in the arts of other coastal peoples (Roy 1992, 42).   PM

Provenance: Philip Sanfield, Detroit

7 EGUNGUN HEADDRESS

Carved by Oniyide Adugbologe of Abeokuta

Yoruba, Nigeria

Wood, pigment

h. 59.7 x 32.4 cm

(23 1/2 x 12 3/4 in.)

Faxon Collection

This mask belongs to the category of Yoruba images known as *egungun*. Egungun masks appear at funerals and at annual festivals to perform the essential function of controlling the relationship between the living and the dead. The seven-day performance of egungun may follow a recent death, but a lengthy and more elaborate festival, lasting as long as fourteen days, is held annually in November. Through the agency of the mask, the spirits of the deceased come to life at a time when the community venerates and remembers them.

Significant regional variations exist in egungun masquerade, with three varieties identified in the Oyo area—*alubata*, *idomole*, and *onidan*. This mask, related to the alubata type of performance, features an anthropomorphized rabbit's head.

The artist is Oniyide Adugbologe, from the southern Yoruba town of Abeokuta. He is known to have lived between 1870 and 1949, and the mask is believed to have been carved around 1925.

Elements characteristic of egungun from the Abeokuta area are the hourglass-shaped pressure drum and small medicine gourds arranged along the hairline; the bulging eyes and very prominent facial scars; and an expressionistic face featuring exposed front teeth. The painted bearded face adds to the dramatic effect of the image. The mask's elaborate coiffure takes the form of a pair of oversized, upwardly erect ears, which identify it as belonging to the *erin* category.

Yet, no matter how attractive the carved mask may be, it is considered less important than its cloth costume. The spectacular costuming that would normally embellish the mask is missing here. The creation of pieces for the masquerades requires the combined efforts of a sculptor and a tailor, as well as an especially large financial investment. So vital is the apparel of the masker that its production is not only preceded by divination, it is secret. Sacrifices performed during the egungun masquerade are perceived as ultimately being directed to the cloth outfit (Wolff 1982, 67). When not in use, the costume serves as a shrine to the spirits of the dead, a further indication that the cloth indeed is the mask.   NQ

Provenance: Franklin Family Collection, Los Angeles, California

8 SEATED FIGURE

Dogon, Mali
Wood
h. 54 cm (21¹/₄ in.)
Anonymous Loan

The Dogon inhabit a harsh land of sandy plateaus and stone cliffs in Mali known as the Bandiagara Escarpment. Over the past five hundred years this has been a place of refuge for a number of ethnic groups fleeing from war or cultural hegemony, including the Dogon who arrived from the Mande area in southwest Mali in the fifteenth century. Cultural unity was established between the original inhabitants and the Dogon-Mande settlers in the seventeenth and eighteenth centuries, but even today the people identified as Dogon are comprised of many diverse ethnic groups (Ezra 1988, 15; Leloup 1988, 44-46).

The Dogon have a complex system of cosmology and mythology to explain the origin of human beings. Many figural works have been identified as representations of the primordial couple who is said to have founded the Dogon people.

A sculpture such as this may represent one of the Dogon ancestors; however, it has also been suggested that the images are of the patrons who commissioned the works. A sculpture is usually commissioned after a solution has not been found for problems such as illness or infertility, and sacrifices on a standard altar have proven ineffective. A blacksmith may then be paid to carve a figure in the form of the client, to which new sacrifices will be performed. The play of horizontals and verticals, repre-senting the union of femininity and masculinity, and the intricately incised herringbone patterns are typical of much Dogon art. Despite stylistic similarities among such figures, the idea is that an individual is being portrayed, and the work is not a common cultural representation of an ancestor (van Beek 1988, 58; Leloup 1994, 158).

The Dogon statues may sometimes depict the client in a state that he or she still aspires to attain. For example, a figure seated on a stool indicates a person who desires to be in harmony with the world. A seated male may represent the authority he hopes to one day hold. In the case of this seated female statue, the figures she sits upon may indicate children, alluding to her desire to raise a strong family (van Beek 1988, 63).

This sculpture was probably placed on an altar to support the spirits of the ancestors and to facilitate the interaction between humans and the supernatural world. The darkened areas and rough surface indicate the use of sacrificial materials such as blood or millet porridge, which may have been poured over the sculpture during the performance of rituals. Other sculptures of similar form were displayed on rooftop terraces of the deceased during the funerals of influential men in the community. It is unlikely that this piece was used for such a purpose, as the surface shows evidence of sacrificial use.   TS

Provenance: John Friede, New York; Merton Simpson, New York

9 BOWL-BEARING FIGURE

Luba, Zaire

Wood

h. 38.4 cm (15¹/₈ in.)

Private Collection

Among the Luba of Zaire, political power and social authority are shared between the king or chief, the semi-secret *Budye* association, and those diviners who practice spirit possession. The interrelations between the three are complex and intertwined, with each branch of authority gaining legitimacy and sanction both through its connections with the others and with the ancestral spirits associated with the founding ideologies of the society. Fundamental to each is the concept of spirit possession and reincarnation, which confers legitimacy to individuals by linking them with those important personages of the past instrumental in the formation and expansion of the Luba kingdoms (Nooter 1991, 292).

The fine figural carvings long admired in the West were the prerogatives of these branches of social authority, suggesting an important link between sculptural arts and power. Significant in this regard is the prevalence of the female image, for although the Luba are patrilineal, women fulfill essential roles in both the political and cosmological realms. Perceived as uniquely suited for communication with the spiritual world, women are members of Budye (whose founder is generally perceived as female) and are also frequently diviners (Nooter 1991, passim). In the past, they served as ambassadors and emissaries to client chiefdoms, often marrying the ruler and thus strengthening the ties between villages. Perhaps most significantly, deceased rulers are believed to reincarnate in the body of a woman, who then assumes essentially autonomous rule of the king's former village and serves as an important advisor to the new ruler (Nooter 1984, 4-5).

Because of these complex associations between women and power, female sculptural images convey multiple iconographic references and were sometimes shared by the different branches of sociopolitical authority. Pieces depicting a woman holding a bowl before her are believed to have originally been the prerogative of possession diviners and were later appropriated by kings and chiefs, underscoring the close association between rulers and divination (Nooter 1991, 211). This association, detailed in the shared genesis myths, was established at the very founding of the Luba kingdoms when the first king was educated and protected by a diviner-priest.

Through spirit possession and reincarnation, these founding personages are manifest in the present, sanctioning rulership.

Bowl-bearing figures were important in the investiture of new rulers. During the ceremonies, the king would be smeared with kaolin to signify his completion of the purification rites necessary for the spiritual sanction of his rule. The white clay was then given to the king as a symbol of his ties to his predecessors, and the bowl was taken to the ruler's home village, where it was carefully guarded against theft (Roy 1992, 169, citing Reefe 1981, 91). In this context, the female figure may therefore be suggestive of the reincarnated spirits of past rulers. Alternatively, she may refer to the ruler's spirit-wife, who holds before her the sacred treasure bowl containing the relics of the previous king, just as the female relation of the founding king was believed to have guarded his important remains (Nooter 1991, 262).

These sculpted insignia were so important as a symbol of legitimacy that kings had to protect them against theft by rivals and immediately commission replacements in the event of loss. Additionally, rulers would often request copies of their finer pieces for gifts to client chiefs, thereby assuring continuing loyalty and dependence. More recently, a Catholic mission in the Mwanza region, where this piece is thought to have originated, commissioned several copies of bowl-bearing figures. However, a number of earlier pieces are known to exist as well, and the aesthetic accomplishment, fine patina, and worn facial features of this example suggest that it belongs to that group (de Maret, Dery, and Murdoch 1973, 13).

In the divination context, bowl-bearing figures performed multiple functions. Diviners used them as receptacles for the kaolin and herbs that they administered to clients as medicinal remedies for a variety of ailments. Additionally, the figures had oracular powers, communicating important information about a person's guilt or innocence in judicial cases. If judged innocent, the accused was smeared with the white clay held within the bowl (Nooter 1991, 212). Because of the association between kaolin and ritual purification, the diviner would also apply the substance to himself and to the sculpted image to facilitate communication with the spiritual realm (Nooter 1991, 106). The female figure underscores these links with the spiritual world, as she is sometimes interpreted as Mijibu'a Kalenga, the first Luba divination priest who is believed to reincarnate through

possession diviners. Alternatively, she has been interpreted as the wife of the diviner's possession spirit (Nooter 1991, 211).

While the female figure is the prevalent motif in Luba sculpture, maternity figures are almost unknown. The figural treatment here, with the lid of the bowl conceived as a secondary female figure, may or may not be intended as a maternal group. In other Luba arts, such as caryatid stools and neck-rests, dual female figures are occasionally rendered. Most Luba informants interpret these examples as references to a particularly important pair of twin tutelary spirits (Nooter 1991, 270). Therefore, while the slightly diminutive size of the lid figure in this example is suggestive of a child, it may perhaps refer instead to these twin spirits.

The finely textured surface decoration is characteristic of Luba sculpture and represents scarification. Although rarely practiced today, scarification was an essential attribute for women in the past, without which they were considered unsuitable for marriage. More importantly, the sexual desirability that scarification enhanced also conferred heightened spiritual powers, which made certain women particularly well suited for communication with the other world and facilitated important transmissions of power (Nooter 1991, 240). Patterns varied regionally and through time, but many designs were emulated over vast areas, and the more prevalent patterns were named. The triangular motif apparent on the rim of this figure's bowl is called *nkaka,* or pangolin. Appearing also on the beaded headdresses worn by diviners and Budye association members during possession rituals, the pattern replicates the pangolin's scales, which were valued for their strength and durability (Nooter 1991, 255). The prevalence of this motif in these three contexts thus underscores the complex association between rulership, divination, and Budye ritual, an association which is based in the essential role of spirit possession in Luba society.   PM

Provenance: Marc Felix, Brussels

⑩ **ESHU FIGURE (ODOSU)**

Yoruba, Nigeria

Wood, leather

15.9 x 14 cm (6¹/₄ x 5¹/₂ in.)

The Collection of Charles, Gail, and Lyndsay McGee

Despite centuries of contact with other peoples, the Yoruba of Nigeria and the Republic of Benin have maintained their own distinctive world view for nearly a millennium. While Christianity and Islam have found a significant number of adherents, many elements of traditional religious belief and practice still remain.

Probably the most important of these is the belief in the power of divination to reveal the sources of illness, strife, and suffering in the community. Although several forms of divination are practiced by the Yoruba, by far the most respected and widely used is *Ifa*, an ancient system governed by the *orisha* (deity) Orunmila, and practiced by ritual specialists known as *babalawos*. The divination process is not unlike the I Ching: through the manipulation of sixteen palm nuts, a series of marks are made in wood dust upon a special tray (the *opon Ifa*), corresponding to specific sections of a corpus of verses. The Ifa verses contain parables and prescriptions, the former to help identify the source of the client's problem, and the latter to provide the solution, which always entails a sacrifice to the appropriate orisha.

The concept of sacrifice is essential in Yoruba thinking because it suggests the interdependence that exists between humans and the orishas. Like one's ancestors, the orishas take an active interest in the affairs of the living and possess the power to effect transformations in one's circumstances. When properly acknowledged through prayer, ritual, and sacrifice, the orishas bestow blessings upon their followers, but can wreak havoc if ignored.

In the Yoruba cosmos, it is Eshu-Elegba and Orunmila who facilitate the communication between the earthly and spiritual realms essential for maintaining an often precarious balance between opposing forces. The Messenger, the Trickster, and the Divine Enforcer, Eshu-Elegba is the orisha of chance and change. As countless myths and *oriki* (praise songs) suggest, his is a contradictory nature that serves as a potent reminder that circumstances can and do change constantly.

While Orunmila is responsible for revealing the orishas' wishes through divination, it is Eshu who actually relays the information. So closely is he associated with Ifa that it is he who is depicted on the top of the opon Ifa, facing the babalawo, and thus watching over the divination process. Because the diviner always orients himself toward an open doorway or a path, Eshu's position at the top of the wooden tray reinforces his role as messenger, for he stands at the road leading from the orishas to humans (M. Drewal 1977, 47). Indeed, Eshu is always associated with entryways and crossroads, a liminal figure perched at the boundary between the earthly and spiritual realms.

This small figure is probably an *odosu,* an image of Eshu that is placed between the diviner's tray and the client. Like the face on the opon Ifa, the odosu stands as a sentinel over the divination process. He is sometimes replaced by a seventeenth palm nut resting upon a ring of cowry shells (Bascom 1969, 28). Although many odosu show only the deity's head, this example depicts the full figure, kneeling and blowing a whistle. This pose frequently appears on the dance wands held by Eshu's devotees in possession rituals, and its supplicant posture is, in Yoruba thinking, the appropriate position for addressing the orishas (Drewal, Pemberton, and Abiodun 1989, 111). Similarly, his whistle-blowing may be interpreted as calling the attention of the deities (Drewal, Pemberton, and Abiodun 1989, 27).

Eshu's ability to see into both realms is frequently suggested by the inclusion of an additional face at the base of his distinctive hair style. The second face is interpreted as that of a dignified elder, while the primary face may be viewed as that of an impertinent youth. These faces suggest one of the many dualities in Eshu's character, for he is both the first-born and the youngest of the orishas, embodying the wisdom of the aged and the capriciousness of youth, and partaking of the privileges of both (Westcott 1962, 341).

The long, pointed hair style shown here is an important feature of Eshu's iconography. In Yoruba thinking, long hair suggests power, strength, and libidinous energy and is worn only by those who, like hunters and priests, embody or can control these forces (Wescott 1962, 348). In many Eshu sculptures, the hair style is depicted as a phallus, suggestive of the unbridled virility with which Eshu was rewarded by Olodumare, the creator god, for having performed the necessary sacrifices during a time of great crisis (Thompson 1994, 229).

The small projections at the base of Eshu's hair represent tiny calabashes that are used to hold important medicines, which heighten a person's spiritual efficacy. Their placement is reminiscent of the Yoruba practice of inserting medicines into the scalp of an orisha devotee, which serves to attract the deity and thus facilitate its possession of the initiate during a trance. The calabashes draw attention to the figure's

Among the Gurunsi populations residing in the grassland regions, carved masks generally represent "the social forces of the village" as opposed to masks made of leaves and grasses, which are said to impersonate nature spirits. Masks make spirits come to life while sculptures make spirits visible to humans (Roy 1987, 40).

The rectilinear decoration of the flat facial plane of this mask is interrupted by the high relief depiction of a human face. Masks have apotropaic functions, guarding families and communities, and may also yield the benefits of sound health, fertility, and material well-being if given the requisite ritual attention. Masks are generally featured in village cleansing ceremonies and funerals of elders, and some are integral to initiations of young people into adults. The dry season is the time most marked by masquerades.

The bushcow or buffalo motif is pervasive in the sculpture of West Africa's savannah. Among the Gurunsi groups, the style represents one of several animal masks. All the known examples share three common traits: painted geometric red, black, and white decorations, such as a checkerboard and lines; use of a plank to give the mask a flat, disk-shaped, and vertical configuration; and the emphasis on the bushcow. This mask vaguely resembles the Sakrobundi mask that was employed in the nineteenth century anti-witchcraft cult among the Bron, Kulango, and related peoples of the Bondoukou region of Côte d'Ivoire. It is possible that the Gurunsi may have originated the mode in their homeland in northern Ghana and central Burkina Faso. Their cultural influence may have percolated south and into central Côte d'Ivoire where increasingly more rounded versions of bushcow masks are known amoung the Baule and related groups.   NQ

Provenance: L. Segy, New York

head, which contains his *ase,* or power to make things happen (M. Drewal 1977, 43).

The leather straps attached to the figure probably once held cowrie shells. As an ancient form of currency, cowries are symbolic of the wealth that Eshu can bring to those who follow the orisha's wishes. They are also evocative of his ties to the marketplace, a tenuous world where fortunes can be quickly made or lost (Pemberton 1975, 25). As an inhabitant of the crossroads, the point of divergent paths, Eshu is so closely associated with the world of trade that most markets contain a shrine devoted to him.

PM

⑪ BUSHCOW MASK

Gurunsi, Burkina Faso, or Ghana

Wood, black and white pigment

111.8 x 58.4 cm

(44 x 23 in.)

The Collection of Sophie Pearlstein

This mask's painted checkerboard pattern and sweeping, near-circular horned superstructure places it within a broad class of sculptures found in a wide geographical area extending from as far north as central Burkina Faso and westward into north-central Côte d'Ivoire. This example may be attributed to a number of related ethnic groups collectively known as Gurunsi, namely the Nuna, Nunuma, Sisala, and Winiama who live in geographically contiguous areas extending into northern Ghana. Of the Gurunsi groups, the Nuna, Winiama, and Lela are the chief producers of art.

⑫ SEATED FEMALE FIGURE WITH CHILDREN

Carved by Kofi Ndri from Djina-Ngassokro (b. 1910)

Baule or Agni

Côte d'Ivoire

Wood

57.2 x 22.2 x 21.6 cm

(22¹/₂ x 8³/₄ x 8¹/₂ in.)

Faxon Collection

Female figures are commonly carved by the Baule and other groups of southeastern Côte d'Ivoire for use in divination rites. While these figures are most commonly depicted standing (representing "spirit mates" or other intermediaries between the human and spirit realms), seated figures, usually found on Akan-style stools, exist as well. Carved by the Baule and Lagoon peoples, they have been referred to as ancestor spirits or nature spirits. Their use seems to have been phased out in the early twentieth century (Phillips 1995, fig. 5.111).

Although the stools are Akan in form, the figure is not and points to the assimilation by the Baule of some Akan styles. In fact, there is evidence of the assimilation of Akan people, culture, and artistic traditions into Baule society since at least the eighteenth century (Vogel 1977, 17). Stools for both groups are central elements in ancestral shrines, serving as the location for offerings made to deceased ancestor spirits (Vogel 1977, 179).

It is not unusual to have a shrine maintained in honor of twins during their lifetimes found in close proximity to ancestor stools (Vogel 1977, 176). This sculpture may be related to twins in some way, for on the lap of the main figure are two smaller ones. While this may be a reference to a spirit and devotees, or to a mother and children, it is possible the piece may have been intended to serve as both a twin and an ancestral commemoration.

As nature spirits or *asie usu*, Baule carved seated figures function similarly to the standing spirit figures and are believed to cause misfortunes in hunting and farming or to cause an individual to fall into a trance and act in a dangerous manner. When this

happens, the person is said to have departed from civilization and wandered into the bush. Like spirit spouses, asie usu are carved in the form of beautiful humans. They have scarifications and stylized coiffures, both signs of civilization (Vogel 1977, 169).

Asie usu are thought to be grotesque and inhuman in appearance. Carved representations, however, are made beautiful as a way to attract the spirits and control their destructive powers. If the figures were not made appealing, the spirits might be offended and refuse to "sit" on them. In fact, the carved figures are often described as asie usu "stools" because the nature spirits sit on them to be tamed. The figures are acknowledged and revered, as are the spirit mates,

so that misfortune will not befall the owner. It is hoped that a spirit will be confined to the stool, signifying that "the wild, uncontrolled bush spirit has been tamed and brought to the village; his once-destructive energies will now work for the good of his host" (Vogel 1977, 169).   LBH

Provenance: Reynold Kerr, New York

⑬ SEATED FIGURE

Malinke, Mali

Wood

h. 58.4 cm (23 in.)

Anonymous Loan

The striking similarities between Bamana and Malinke sculpture demonstrate the cross-cultural exchange between these two Mande groups, which share a common history and today live side by side in many areas of southern Mali. More is known about the Bamana, and thus far Malinke sculpture has been discussed only in relationship to Bamana form and style. This Malinke work appears to contain elements from the figurative sculpture of both the Jo and Gwan societies of the Bamana.

The Gwan and Jo societies are closely affiliated, and in many villages the rituals of the two are often interconnected to some degree (Imperato 1983, 33). While the Jo ceremonies focus on agricultural fecundity, the Gwan rituals concentrate on problems of human fertility and childbearing. Women concerned with these issues may attend annual Gwan ceremonies, making sacrifices on the threshold of a house where groups of figures are enshrined. During the ceremonies, the figures are brought out of the shrine for public display. On such occasions they are washed, oiled, and then adorned with loincloths, headbands, and beads contributed by the women of the village. Those women who have sought the powers of Gwan and consequently succeed in having children make additional sacrifices and dedicate their offspring to the society and may name them after the sculptures used by the association (Ezra 1988, 22).

These groups of enshrined sculptures normally consist of a seated mother and child (the *Gwandusu* in the Gwan association), a father, and a variety of other male and female figures (Ezra 1987, 22, 23). On occasion the Gwandusu are represented without children, but with swollen abdomens, alluding to their pregnant condition (Imperato 1983, 49). The most important figure in the group is usually seated on a stool and can be identified by this place of honor (Ezra 1983, 149).

Although the exact function of this Malinke carving is not known, the figure's swelling belly and seated, frontal pose comply with the central elements of the Bamana Gwandusu. It is certainly possible that this figure depicts a Gwandusu, or was used for a similar purpose. However, the flat geometric planes of the figure's face, the rectilinear nature of the chest, and the flattened hands are more reminiscent of the style found on Jo society sculptures than the usually more rounded forms of the Gwandusu. These attributes would seemingly preclude the figure's use in Gwan society rites (Imperato 1983, 49). This apparent inclusion of both Jo and Gwan sculptural styles may demonstrate a strong interchange of stylistic ideas between the Bamana and the Malinke, or it could indicate even more specific regional styles at work.   TS

Provenance: James Willis, San Francisco, California

⑭ MASK (EKPO IDIOK)

Ibibio, Nigeria
Wood, pigment,
cloth, raffia
h. 30.5 cm (mask only);
48.3 cm (including cloth),
(12 in.; 19 in.)
Private Collection,
Birmingham, Michigan

In precolonial times, the Ekpo society functioned as an important governing body for the Ibibio people of southern Nigeria, assisting village chiefs with the collection of taxes, the enforcement of order, and the punishment of wrongdoers. Although largely a social and entertainment organization now, the society is occasionally called upon to fulfill some of its traditional roles. "Ekpo" translates literally as "ghost," and is used also to refer to ancestors, which helps to explain the tremendous power wielded by the association in former times.

The Ibibio believe that the ancestors control the actions and the fate of their descendants and disobeying their wishes brings misfortune to individuals and to the community. The Ekpo society thus enforces social order on behalf of, and through the sanction of, the ancestors (Offiong 1984, 79).

Essential to the society's functioning in the past was the use of masks, whose appearances served as temporary incarnations of the ancestors among the living. The hidden identity of the masquerader was imperative, for while costumed he was not held responsible for his actions, which in turn allowed for the meting out of justice, even to his relations (Offiong 1984, 120). Masks were usually stored in the society's meeting house at the outskirts of the village, an appropriate location since the nearby

bush had been used for burial ground and was therefore regarded as the place of the spirits.

Broadly speaking, Ekpo masks fall into two categories: *ekpo mfon*, which translates as "good" or "beautiful," and *ekpo idiok*, which is "bad" or "ugly." This dichotomy reflects the Ibibio view of death, wherein those who led morally upright lives are afforded the possibility of reincarnation, while those who were evil in life are fated to remain wandering ghosts forever (Messenger 1973, 119-20). The beautiful masks therefore represent prominent ancestors, who have returned to bestow favor upon their descendants, while the others are the restless spirits of malfeasants who serve as a reminder to behave well.

This piece, with its black color, distorted features, and attachment of raffia netting and rags, is clearly of the latter category. Masks of this type may also combine animal attributes or the symptoms of blindness, yaws, or leprosy to create equally unsettling visages. These characteristics suggest that disfigurement or disease is a punishment for those who fail to behave.

Their unkempt costumes and their wild, unpredictable behavior were as important as their forbidding features. The masqueraders would rush erratically through the village, clad in raffia strands or strips of dirty cloth, climbing trees and roofs, destroying property, and speaking unintelligibly. They rubbed their exposed limbs with charcoal, the black heightening their connection with death. From a wide raffia belt hung a large machete, and rattles on their ankles announced their presence in advance. In contrast to the eager anticipation felt at the appearance of the beautiful masks, the ugly type solicited fear and trepidation from the village. Since the spirits of each type ventured back to the realm of the living at different times, the two kinds of masks were never seen together. Generally, the beautiful masks appeared first, and then retired before the appearance of the others at night (Messenger 1973, 122).

PM

Provenance: Franklin Family Collection, Los Angeles, California

ⓘ FIGURINE

Chokwe, Angola

Wood, fabric,

beads, metal

h. 17.2 cm (6 ³/₄ in.)

Anonymous Lender

In the mid-nineteenth century, increasing European demand for ivory and rubber allowed the Chokwe peoples of Angola to dramatically increase their wealth and power, precipitating a sizable expansion of their territories (Koloss 1990, 13). However, economic and political reversals in the latter half of the century caused by disease, over-hunting, and increased European presence in the country's interior, resulted in great migrations into northern Angola and Zaire, where the Chokwe settled in small villages in the lands of foreign peoples (Serpa Pinto 1881, 234-35, cited in Bastin 1992, 67). While they maintained many of their religious beliefs and political structures, their art was subtly transformed by the influences of their neighbors and the changes in their condition.

The most important of these was the decline in political authority of their chiefs. The arts of this period and region, dubbed the "Style of the Expansion," often lack the awesome presence associated with classical Chokwe court arts (Bastin 1982, 253).

The finest of the Expansion Style thrones and figures, however, achieve a remarkable grace and harmony in their form, as this small figure illustrates. The muscular limbs and massive extremities so common in the arts of the original lands are here replaced by a more delicately linear treatment, while the torso is reduced to a broad cylinder. There is an angularity to both the arms and face, which contrasts with the rigid verticality of the torso and pose. Only the exquisitely detailed treatment of the hair style, with its curved form and carefully incised plaits, recalls the more rounded treatment found in examples from the original Chokwe regions.

The Chokwe commissioned some of the carved figures to commemorate their dead family members. Hair styles and scarification of the deceased were faithfully recorded, as in the *masoji,* or "tears" indicated here by parallel lines beneath the eyes (Bastin 1982, 72, 79). Following an expedition to Angola in 1930, the German scholar Hermann Baumann reported that the figures were kept under their owners' beds and brought out in times of trouble to receive propitiatory sacrifices. In this manner, the ancestors were attracted to the sculptures, ensuring the restoration of good fortune (Baumann 1935, 196, cited in Koloss 1990, 54).

Baumann collected a somewhat similar figure, now in the Berlin Museum für Völkerkunde, reportedly depicting the owner's deceased sister (Bastin 1982, figure 100; Koloss 1990, figure 33). Like the present example, the Berlin piece wears necklaces of glass trade beads and has a small depression in the middle of the torso. She, too, has an elegant, plaited coiffure, which includes a carved representation of a beaded headband. Both figures are rather small (the Berlin piece measures eight and one-quarter inches) in comparison with most Chokwe figures, which often exceed a foot in height. When originally illustrated by Baumann in 1935, the Berlin figure also had a waistcloth, which has since been removed (Bastin 1982, 169).

While the inclusion of beads and copper ornaments, as well as the brass tacks on the Detroit example, suggest wealth and prestige, the depression in the torso has not been explained. Chokwe figures occasionally include small horns inserted in the head, or, as in the Berlin figure, carried in the hand,

into which magical substances were placed. It is possible that the hole in the torso functioned similarly, as in Kongo and Songye figures. Indeed, the facial treatment of the piece, with the strongly triangular jaw and closely-set eyes, is reminiscent of many Songye power figures, which may suggest a northern origin for the work.

The figure's gesture, with arms raised and hands placed at her chest, is sometimes rendered on effigies of chiefs. Termed *taci,* the pose is symbolic of power and wealth (Bastin 1982, 112). A number of Chokwe female figures display insignia or gestures associated with rulers. This tendency has not been fully explained, but it may suggest that these female figures portray either the chief's mother or his principal wife. In a matrilineal society, women are important for the continuation of the chiefly line, and among the Chokwe, they often wielded considerable influence at court (Bastin 1982, 46).

PM

Provenance: Marc Felix, Brussels

⑯ RAM MASK (BOLO)

Bobo, Burkina Faso
Wood
44.5 x 33.7 cm
(17¹/₂ x 13¹/₄ in.)
Faxon Collection

Burkina Faso, formerly Upper Volta, is inhabited by a variety of ethnic groups including the Bobo and Bwa. The Bobo live to the west of the Bwa, with whom they are often confused. The Bobo are actually a blend of ancient peoples numbering around 110,000. Although the majority live in Burkina Faso, many also inhabit an area that extends into southern Mali, and therefore have commonalities with the Bamana.

The Bobo are agriculturalists whose social and political organization centers around a council of male elders from all family/clan lineages. These lineages are believed to be descended from a common ancestor, called

wakoma, relating to the Bobo word for "house." In Bobo religion and mythology, the god Wuro created the world in pairs of balanced, opposing forces: "man/spirits, male/female, village/bush, domesticated/ wild, culture/nature, safety/danger, hot/cold, farmer/blacksmith" (Roy 1987, 318). The guiding principal of Bobo moral and social behavior is the belief that human actions can disrupt this fragile balance and create chaos in the world. The Bobo also believe that the first man created by Wuro was the blacksmith, with the farmer created second as the smith's companion.

Bobo farmers usually use masks made of leaves and fiber, and sometimes cloth. But they can acquire the right to masks with wooden heads. Wooden masks must be carved by a blacksmith who, as the first human created is at liberty to use masks

made of all four materials—leaves, fiber, cloth and wood. Bobo masks appear at harvest time, during male initiations, and in funeral and burial rites. In addition to sacred masks created for ritual purposes, the Bobo carve masks for entertainment, called bolo. Typically these are helmet masks, representing people and animals such as the antelope, ram, rooster and monkey, worn with fiber costumes and decorated with bright yellow, red, and blue enamel paints and found in the possession of farmers.

The ram's head mask illustrated here belongs to this type. Although there are no traces of pigment or the fiber attachments, this mask is virtually the same as one illustrated (figure 300) in Roy's *Art of the Upper Volta Rivers* (1990) and may, in fact, be by the same hand.   LR

Provenance: William Wright, New York

TO PROTECT AND DEFEND

A chief's protective charm: the imported chevron beads are prestige items, while the squirrel tail is considered to be spiritually efficacious. Shai, Dangme, Ghana 1987.

MUCH ART IS PRODUCED TO APPEASE,

counteract, or control the substantial group of largely negative forces that dominate the African world. Witchcraft and sorcery occupy positions of central importance among these powers because they are intimately linked both to individual and communal prosperity and well-being (Mbiti 1991). The belief in witchcraft suggests that certain individuals are endowed with the capability to affect others "adversely by means of unseen agencies working in the unseen world, . . . an innate and often undetected ability . . . to work mystically on other individuals in a biological way" (Siroto 1973, 245). Sorcery, in contrast, is a form of occult power that is controlled and deliberate (Leach 1961). To counteract the inherent supernatural powers of both witchcraft and sorcery, it is thus necessary to create and use a range of tools and practices (Siroto 1973).

To defend against witchcraft powers, the work of art may include in its design an arsenal of potent attributes combined in a way to enable it to perform three key functions: to protect against attacks; to heal or to restore normalcy; and last, to destroy. Conceptually, therefore, most anti-witchcraft images and practices incorporate elements that are antithetical to the negative forces being confronted (Siroto 1973, 244).

However, art's role is not always intended to be combative and reactionary. Sometimes the aim is to secure life by coaxing and appeasing dangerous spiritual forces, rendering their powers less destructive or even beneficial. This strategy of containment underlies the Yoruba *gelede* masquerade performances that seek to acknowledge the harmful and constructive potential of these invidious powers with which Yoruba women are naturally endowed and to tap into those capabilities for positive ends.

In the same way that village lineage and integrity are protected with the aid of the preserved remains of ancestors, so individual prosperity, achievement, and survival is enhanced through the agency of certain personal art objects. Such works of art would shield its owner from both known and unforeseen dangers. These potent tutelary devices may be essentially private and personal or communally owned. Frequently, the composed form centralizes and captures the essence of the patron's uniqueness.

Having foreknowledge of events to come emboldens one to act decisively. Thus, for some African cultures every important activity is preceded by some inquiry into its outcome. It is for this reason that the Yoruba, for instance, hold diviners in such high esteem.

African peoples approach this issue of selfhood from a variety of perspectives. First, is to resort to divination or other means of prognostication to foretell the future. Second, is to insure the sanctity of one's being and how one's individuality relates to that of others and to the general spiritual environment. Third, is to use images to project the self and to enable one to achieve prosperity. Baule, Atyie, and Ebrie spirit spouse figures, Yoruba *ille ori* ("house of the head"), and *Igbo ikenga* all incarnate extraordinary spiritual powers that protect a person's spiritual integrity, which many African peoples consider significant in insuring one's prosperity.   NQ

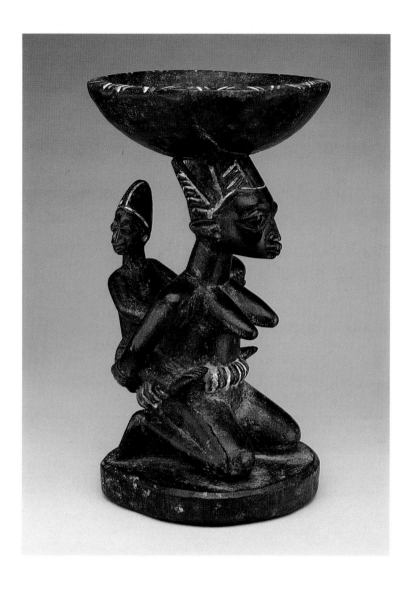

The woman and child reflect the role of women in Yoruba society. Women are considered soothing, indulgent, patient, enduring, and nurturers of children. Women are also considered to be intermediaries with the gods, whose spiritual power is bound to biological reality and the practice of raising children (M. Drewal 1986, 62). The elaborate detail given to the head of the woman and child underscores the importance of the head as spiritual center in Yoruba religious traditions.

⑰ IFA DIVINATION BOWL

Yoruba, Nigeria
Wood, pigment
h. 22.2 x 12.7 cm
(8 ³/₄ x 5 in.)
Anonymous Lender

Sculptures such as this bowl were made to hold the sixteen sacred palm nuts used during consultation with Ifa, the system of secret religious knowledge of the Yoruba people of southwestern Nigeria. The Yoruba city of Ifè is claimed as the origin of Ifa divination. In the traditional histories, it is believed that all of the original Yoruba kingdoms were the descendants of the sixteen sons of the first king of Ifè and divine creator of the universe at Ifa.

Orunmila, a son of Olorun, the owner of heaven, is considered the inventor of the Ifa oracle. When Olorun saw that humans were suffering on earth, he sent Orunmila to teach people about the *orisha*, the gods that act upon all aspects of life. Each god, or orisha, has its own influences and particular preferences in the ritual performances made in their honor, including music, color, dance, rhythm, symbols, and sacrifices. Orunmila is the god of oracles whose divine knowledge of destiny is consulted through Ifa.

To consult with Ifa, sixteen palm nuts, called *ikin Ifa*, are removed from a receptacle, such as this one, and tossed from one hand to the other by the diviner to determine the oral verses essential to the divination process. Ifa is consulted for guidance throughout the life of any Yoruba who clings to traditional religious beliefs and especially during times of crisis or sickness, at the birth of a child, before a marriage, and before important political appointments are made.

A similar Ifa divination bowl, attributed to the Southern Ekiti area and dated from the nineteenth century, and similar to this one, has been described as "a marvelous merging of religious and domestic actions. The devotee kneels before the gods in supplication, her face composed and purposeful in its concentration, while, at one and the same moment, she holds and adjusts the child on her back" (H. Drewal et al. 1989, 196).

In Yoruba culture, spirituality and artistic representation are in many cases inextricably linked. In a detailed account of aesthetics in Yoruba culture, Robert Farris Thompson explains that generally the Yoruba do not attempt to create artistic works of exact likeness to the human form. He claims that "there can be something sinister about absolute mimesis" (Thompson 1973, 32). This may be why certain aspects of this sculpture may seem constrained or even rigid. The Yoruba do, however, consider clarity of form and line crucial elements to a successful work of art, thus the lucidity of the facial features and the sharp, almost geometric depiction of the child and mother's poses.   ON/NQ

Provenance: Charles Fox, San Francisco, California

18 DIVINATION IMPLEMENT (ITOMBWA)

Lele, Zaire

Wood

l. 34.3 cm (13¹/₂ in.)

Private Collection, Birmingham, Michigan

Throughout Zaire, but particularly in the area dominated by the Kuba people, a variety of divining implements often called friction oracles *(Itombwa)* are used to locate sorcerers and to find cures for diseases. Highly stylized anthropomorphic and zoomorphic representations, which were flattened on the top, were equipped with separate flat round knobs (looking a bit like chess pawns) that are rubbed by a diviner across the top of the implement after it has been lubricated with oil. As he rubs the implement with the knob, he chants the names of people,

places, and magical substances. As the oil becomes more viscous, the knob eventually sticks coincident with the utterance of a specific name. The oracle is then believed to have "spoken."

The numerous animals depicted on these divining implements are usually selected for their specific traits and their importance to the supernatural world. The warthog depicted here is renowned for its courage and is believed to have special ties to the spirit world. With its sides, decorated with intricate patterns recalling Kuba textile art, it closely resembles an example from the University Museum of Pennsylvania (AF5196), which was collected by Captain C. Blank in the Belgian Congo before 1920 and purchased from W.O. Oldman in 1924.

MK

Provenance: Karl-Ferdinand Schadler

⑲ **POWER FIGURE (NKISI MUTADI)**

Kongo, Zaire
Wood, metal, cloth
29.2 x 31.8 cm
(11 1/2 x 12 1/2 in.)
The Collection of Dede and Oscar Feldman

Minkisi (sing. *nkisi*) are intermediary vehicles through which the living appeal to the spirit world. Most minkisi are created to promote well-being, prosperity, and fertility. The potency of *minkisi* comes from the consecration of spirits and is enhanced by powers obtained from magical substances made from shells, seeds, leaves, horns, soil, nails, animal pelts, and other ingredients applied to the sculpture. Minkisi, which can be owned by groups or individuals, are effective only after they have been ritually activated by an expert, or *nganga.*

This figure is a *nkisi mutadi*, a sculptural form used to appeal to the benevolent powers of local spirits, and is used for divination. The mediating function of nkisi mutadi is indicated by its non-aggressive pose and the presence of white clay or kaolin, which signifies the white skin of the dead. The white pigment may also suggest that this piece belongs to the water class of minkisi that addresses the concerns of women and appeals to the local guardian spirits (MacGaffey 1993, 27, 67). The small scale of the piece may indicate that it was for individual or private use. The application of beads, rags, and metal padlocks around the torso of the figure most likely had personal significance for the client and the ritual specialist who activated the piece.   MLW

Provenance: Marc Felix, Brussels

㉛ **MEDICINE STAFF (OPA OSANYIN)**

Yoruba, Nigeria

Iron

h. 138.4 cm (54¹/₂ in.)

Private Collection

Ornamental iron staffs are used by diviner priests associated with Osanyin, the Yoruba god of herbalism. Because of their vast knowledge of the curative and protective properties of plants, these priests are essential for the physical and mental well-being of their societies. Moreover, this knowledge forms an integral part of Yoruba religious practice, since each god's worship entails the use of specific leaves and herbal preparations. As lord of the forest, then, Osanyin is central to the Yoruba cosmos.

Osanyin's legends describe him as lacking one leg, one arm, and one eye. These injuries were the punishment that Eshu, the trickster god, inflicted for his unwillingness to share the task of healing with the diviner. In another tale, Osanyin is again physically punished with the loss of his deep voice, this time for failing to acknowledge the authority of the god of divination through proper sacrifice. In this reduced state, the once-arrogant Osanyin is now dependent upon the diviner both for speech and for the collection of his leaves (Thompson 1975, 53-54). Osanyin priests use a small, one-legged, one-armed figure that "speaks" in a tiny squeak when consulting with clients. The figure is both a conduit for the god and a reminder to the viewer of the divine retribution that awaits those who anger the gods through selfishness or pride.

Despite his deformities, it is Osanyin who has the power to combat the negative forces that can be marshaled by certain elderly women. These women, affectionately termed "mothers," are believed capable of transforming themselves into birds at night and congregating in trees where they plan sorcerous mischief. Indeed, only with the cooperation of the "mothers" can the herbalist collect his specimens. It is these contradictory roles, as both adversary and assistant, which are suggested by the inclusion of the bird familiars of the "mothers" on the herbalist's staff (Drewal 1977, 11).

The bird at the staff's summit, surrounded by the "mothers," represents the god himself. His superior size and position suggest his power to combat the birds of witchcraft, subduing the "mothers" through the use of special leaves and medicines (Thompson 1975, 58-59). The arrangement also recalls another legend that describes the bird of the god of divination, surrounded by the "mothers" who sought his destruc-

tion. Because of the magical items that he held, he captured their magical powers and rose above them in triumph (Thompson 1975, 59, citing Verger 1965, 171). Significantly, this bird-above-birds motif also appears on many of the beaded crowns worn by Yoruba kings, where it is interpreted as a reference to the king's dependence upon both the control and support of the "mothers" for effective rule. It is the herbalist priests who prepare these crowns for use by inserting special medicines in the peak (Drewal, Pemberton, and Abiodun 1989, 38-39).

A senior diviner has interpreted the inverted cone-shaped images below the birds as particular types of leaves that are folded to enclose protective medicines (Thompson 1975, 56). Beneath these cones are bells which serve to strengthen the force of prayers, and which the diviner may also ring each night before bed to prevent evil visitations. The *agogo* bell, another of the herbalist's emblems, is thought pleasing to the "mothers," and the small bells on the staff may similarly serve to placate them (Thompson 1975, 55-6).

The use of iron for these staffs is also significant. Associated with Ogun, the warrior god, iron is an extremely important material in Yoruba life and ritual, since it is this metal that has allowed for the clearing and cultivation of land, building of cities, and hunting of game. Although hunters are devotees of Ogun, they too honor Osanyin, with whose plants they are also familiar, and both the herbalist and the hunter require Ogun's iron tools to collect their medicines (Thompson 1975, 56). It is not surprising, then, that many herbalist staffs also feature small representations of iron weapons and tools.

Herbalists use these staffs as emblems of their office. Usually planted firmly in the ground outside a doorway, they signal the presence of the diviner inside. They are also believed to guard the entryway against negative forces. Their upright position is essential, for it is connected with the health and well-being of the people (Thompson 1975, 56). In both use and iconography, then, the herbalist staff reveals the potent capacity of its owner to combat witchcraft and restore health and order.   RV/PM

Provenance: Reynold Kerr, New York

㉑ IKENGA FIGURE

Ibo, Nigeria

Wood, pigment

h. 75.6 cm (29³/₄ in.)

Faxon Collection

For the Ibo, wooden statuary is thought to be an active representation of spirits, and it is erected as a means of communication with the spirit world. *Ikenga* shrines and figures, such as this one, signify male potency in the Ibo community. An Ibo's right hand is believed to be the source of his prosperity and survival. It is the right hand that carries his weapons and implements of farming. Consequently the Ibo consider the right hand in need of propitiation if one is to succeed in life. Ikenga figures are kept in private shrines, maintained by men and occasionally by economically successful women (Uche-Okeke 1985, 21-41). Their power is increased by elements connected with warfare, hunting, and farming that refer to social, economic, and spiritual wealth. Customarily, Ikenga images are carved of hardwood from trees such as ikoro or ojilisi, both associated with masculinity. The sculptures are consecrated with offerings of yam, the blood of a rooster, and kola nuts. The figure is privately worshiped and by appealing to the spirit it represents, the owner succeeds in his ventures. So personal is an ikenga that when its owner dies, the figure is either split in two and discarded after the funeral rite or it is kept in the family as a reminder of the individual (Cole and Aniakor 1984, 27).

Often depicted as humans with horns, ikenga figures are rendered in either abstract or highly figurative forms. This figure incorporates aspects of both. Composed of a series of vertically constructed shapes, it emphasizes an incised stool in the center, while symbols of status or lineage are carved in high relief along the cylindrical torso. The primary iconographical element of ikenga is a pair of ram horns. Among the Ibo, the horn is the symbol of masculine power, analogous to aggression and diligence. However, another interpretation regards the upward thrust of the wood atop the head as a pair of open hands showing the Ikenga as pure and the owner's acts as ethically sanctioned by Ibo codes of moral conduct (Aniakor 1973, 9).   MLW

Provenance: Eric Robertson, New York

㉒ RELIQUARY HEAD

Left　*Fang, Gabon*
Wood, metal
h. 25.4 cm (10 in.)
Anonymous Loan

㉓ SEATED RELIQUARY

Right　**FIGURE**

Fang, Gabon
Wood, metal
h. 49.9 cm (19 ²/₃ in.)
Anonymous Loan

Fang heads and figures such as these were made for the *byeri,* a family cult that venerated important ancestors by preserving their remains in reliquary containers (*nsekh byeri*) made of sewn-together pieces of bark. Ancestral status was awarded to founders of lineages, heads of clans and families, and women who displayed extraordinary powers, such as the ability to mother an unusual number of children. The essential remains of these ancestors were their skulls, which were believed to be the locus of an individual's life force. Frequently bones from the arms, legs, and vertebrae were preserved as well. Carved wooden heads and figures (*nlo byeri* or *eyema byeri*), commissioned by families to guard the remains of their ancestors, were attached to reliquary containers by a pole inserted in the back or the neck of the sculpture (Perrois 1990, 42-43).

Fang reliquary carvings functioned as a shield between the relics and possible destructive forces, protecting both the ancestors' remains from intruders and malevolent supernatural forces and vulnerable humans such as the uninitiated, women, and non-family members from the potentially dangerous ancestors.

Only initiated men of the family clan were able to see the byeri relics. During one of the byeri rituals known as *melan,* young men being initiated were given herbal hallucinogens and presented the figural statues as symbolic evocations of their ancestors. In this way the statues were used as instruments to help animate the deceased and to actualize the presence of the clan ancestors. When these statues are removed from the ancestral remains, however, they function only as symbols and not as direct receptacles for the spirits (Perrois and Delage 1990, 50-54).

The Fang were originally a nomadic people, and it has been suggested that the earliest reliquaries consisted only of the easily transported head. The figural form evolved in the nineteenth century only after the Fang established permanent settlements (Tessman 1913, 2, 117-21). Stylistically

there is little variation among the byeri heads, with the exception of the coiffure, which takes on one of three styles: the most common a helmet-wig with ekuma braids, the helmet-wig with a saggital crest, and the transverse chignon. The individual hair styles do not indicate portraits of specific ancestors; rather, the general homogeneity of the reliquary heads suggests that they depict the ideal beauty of all deceased. The hair style on this head appears to represent a saggital crest, which would indicate a male figure (Perrois 1985, 144-46; 1995, 318-19).

The figural sculptures represent beauty through a diverse number of Fang sub-styles with their own specific criteria for beauty, such as a peg-shaped navel, particular coiffures or scarifications, brass decorations, or a bulging forehead (Perrois and Delage 1990, 55). The seated figure with its large bulging forehead, concave heart-shaped face, pursed mouth and exposed teeth, elongated torso, large calves, glossy finish, and brass decorations on the ears and eyes embodies the characteristic elements of the Ntumu style (Perrois and Delage 1990, 114; 1985, 214). The chain connecting the ears was probably part of an elaborate headdress made of eagle and touraco feathers. The reflective copper used for the eyes probably served as more than embellishment, alluding to the figure's ability to watch over the ancestral relics. This figure holds an offering bowl, a relatively uncommon characteristic for a piece in Western collections. Bowls are often removed when the figures are sold to Westerners for they are believed to be the most highly charged area of the carving (Perrois and Delage 1990, 118).　　TS

Provenance:
22. D. Schwob, Brussels
23. Paul Guillaume, Paris

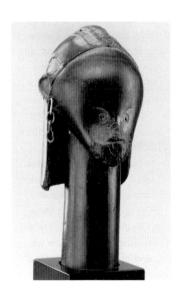

24 25 SONGYE POWER FIGURES (NKISI) In the Songye community, as elsewhere in Africa, *minkisi* (sing. *nkisi*) are mediating vessels containing magical substances that serve as spirit protectors against evil forces. These figures restore and maintain the well-being of owners and possess both benevolent and malevolent functions to ensure balance and continuity within the group. The construction of minkisi is the responsibility of a ritual expert, or *nganga*, who instructs the artist on such matters as specific dimensions and selection of wood for the sculpture. The figure is considered spiritually empty until it has been activated by the ritual expert.

The festival of the new moon is one of the most important public rituals among the Songye. The return of the moon restores health, peace, and fecundity to the land and its people. The ritual context of communal minkisi is associated with the day of the first quarter lunar cycle (*mukapasu*), with the sculptures serving as the focus of proceedings during the festival (Hersak 1985, 134; Mestach 1985, 164). Adorned with all of the protective potency of magical substances, or *bijimba*, the figures are set out to receive a libation of the blood of a rooster and are then anointed with palm oil, manioc flour, or kaolin. Participants in the ceremony similarly apply the white pigment to their faces to purify their souls for the ancestors, symbolizing the connection between the living and the dead. These sacred acts are performed by the nganga and his assistants (male or female), who are also referred to as guardians (*nkunja*).

The smaller of these two figures would have been carried through the village with nkunja manipulating the metal rods on each side of the piece to intimidate those with evil intentions. Immediately thereafter, masqueraders would dance in appreciation of the moon and its benevolent power, which sustains the community. A Kifwebe insignia can be found on the chin of this heavily adorned piece, which places it within the provenance of the masking society

Bwadi Bwa Kifwebe, one of three major secret sects among the Kalebwe sect of the eastern Songye (Mestach 1985, 165). The society's authority is social, economic, and political, and its masqueraders appear at funerary rites, investitures of chiefs, and circumcision and initiation rites, as well as lunar festivals.

In light of its role in the festival of the new moon and the Kifwebe insignia, the Kalebwe figure possesses both a malevolent and benevolent function. It manifests itself as a protective force in the community, maintaining the authority of the Kifwebe society. The scale and form of the figure suggests that the work was commissioned by the Kifwebe for the collective use of the membership.

Allusions to strength, aggression, and male virtues upheld by the Kifwebe are present in additive objects on the Kalebwe piece, including shotgun shells, knives, and lizard skins, which may also refer to the hunt or warfare. The monkey pelt and hawk feathers also represent desired characteristics; the monkey is revered for his shrewdness, while the hawk is associated with swiftness (Hersak 1985, 129, 131).

The larger sculpted figure possesses a solely benevolent and protective function. Its scale and form also imply collective use, but its range perhaps includes those outside of the Kifwebe masking society. As guardian figures, minkisi of this scale were often isolated and housed in the center of the community during the festival, which would explain the addition of a substantial base. The general treatment of the body and patination of the upper torso suggests that this figure was dressed in costume while consecrated. The brass or copper studs on the body and face are believed to augment the strength of the figure because of their association with benevolent ancestral powers. Moreover, brass or copper applied to the face has a specific relationship to lightning, referring to a powerful source that counteracts evil.

**24 POWER FIGURE
(NKISI)**

Songye, Zaire
Wood, fabric, iron, beads
h. 45.7 cm (18 in.)
Private Collection

The goat or antelope horn is one of the most important elements added to these sculptures, symbolizing power, fertility, and fecundity. While on the Kalebwe piece the horn is hung on the side of the figure, it is often placed on top of the head as on the larger nkisi. The symbolic function of the horn on the head is magnified by the magical substances placed inside its cavity, sustaining the figure's spiritual potency. The horn, with its hollow and rigid characteristics, further illustrates the principle of male and female fertility and refers to the cosmology of the lunar rite. The male element is represented by the exterior of the horn, the female by the hollow interior, which is fertilized with *bijimba* (Mestach 1985, 165).

The heads on both pieces are given special sculptural treatment, occupying one-third of the body proportions. In many African societies, the head is thought of as the site of communication with the spirits. Consequently, some minkisi may have secret substances placed on or in the head or are fed through the mouth to maximize spirit interaction (MacGaffey 1993, 65). While the larger figure is not heavily adorned, the amount of attention given to the head in the form of the carved horn, metal nails, and hair treatment suggests the status of the patron or the figure's importance among the Songye. On the Kalebwe nikisi, the painting of the face reflects the symbolic colors of the Kifwebe. Each side of the face is painted red and black. Among the Kifwebe the color black, made from ashes or charcoal, has a neutral role and when used alone has no meaning. However, when placed with white or red, it signifies anger, darkness, and impending danger. The red pigment, made from sandstone or ground fruit, is associated with blood, flesh, and fire and is symbolic of strength, knowledge, and achievement. It also symbolizes witch-craft and ritual murder (Hersak 1985, 68-69; Merriam 1978, 91). Accordingly, the facial coloring indicates the nkisi's purpose to warn and protect.   MLW

Provenance:
24. Marc Felix, Brussels
25. Henri Kamer, Paris; Paul Tishman, New York; Marc and Denyse Ginzberg, New York; Tambaran Gall, New York

㉕ **MALE POWER FIGURE (NKISI)**

Songye, Zaire
Wood, brass tacks,
copper, animal skin
h. 138.4 cm (54¹/₂ in.)
The Detroit Institute of Arts
Founders Society Purchase,
Eleanor Clay Ford Fund
for African Art, New
Endowment Fund,
funds from the Friends
of African and African
American Art, Ralph
Harman Booth Bequest
Fund, funds from L. and R.
Entwistle and Company,
Dennis and Leslie Rogers,
Matilda Wilson, Abraham
Borman Family Fund,
and Mary Martin Semmes
Fund (1995.69)

26 STANDING FIGURE (LEKAT)

Bangwa (Bamenda-Tikar)

Cameroon

Wood

h. 43 in. (109 cm)

Anonymous Loan

Two types of figures intended to ward off evil witchcraft are frequently carved by the Bangwa of western Cameroon—the *njoo* and *lekat*. The njoo tend to be small, with bent arms and legs and anthropomorphic or zoomorphic features. They are often carved very quickly, with no added ornamentation, and placed outside individuals' homes to guard against witches, thieves, and adulterers. Lekat figures,

such as this one, are larger, up to four feet tall, and are carved with greater care than the njoo figures. Rather than simply warning away witches and other criminals, these figures are capable of harming them. When misfortune visits an individual or family, a diviner will attempt to determine who is at fault. That person (or persons) must declare innocence, under oath, in front of the lekat figure. If the accused lies, the figure's powers will be invoked.

The swollen stomach, characteristic of lekat figures, holds medication intended to harm evil-doers inserted through a small panel in the front or back of the torso. The bent arms, with hands extended up to the neck, represent "the attitude of a begging orphan or friendless person" (Brain and Pollock 1971, 129) and are an indication of the curse that will befall the accused.

The Bangwa do not believe that medication can be easily transferred from one carved figure to another, but rather that its powers accumulate over time. Therefore, new anti-witchcraft statues are not commonly carved to replace old ones, and these works are not generally sold outside of the Bangwa society. Their existence in museums and private collections is rare.

More common in outside collections are ancestor statues, which share many similarities to the lekat figures. Sometimes referred to as royal commemorative figures (Harter 1990, 70), they are carved before a ruler's death and are meant to commemorate him. A figure is not supposed to resemble the ruler for whom it was made, though it is designated by that ruler's name.

Royal commemorative sculptures may resemble lekat figures to some degree. They are generally the same height and depict a standing human figure. However, ancestor figures tend to include carved skirts or other royal attributes such as pipes or staffs, which are not found on the lekat objects. The ancestor statues do not usually have the swollen bellies of the lekat figures, nor do they have receptacles in which to place medicine.   LBH

Provenance: Franklin Family Collection, Los Angeles, California

27 GELEDE SOCIETY HELMET MASK

Yoruba Nigeria
Wood
l. 29.2 cm (11¹/₂ in.)
Anonymous Loan

Gelede is a communal masquerade among the western Yoruba in Nigeria. The festival is dedicated to women, particularly elderly women, whose powers are regarded as comparable to those of the gods, other deities, and ancestors. Gelede is performed to show respect to senior women—to honor their powers that contribute to the community's well-being. At the same time, it is meant to appease them so they do not use their power in any destructive ways. The Yoruba people's fear of witchcraft is so strong that they do not dare to mention the term "witches," but use a more respectful term such as "our mothers." Fear and respect of "our mothers" keep the Yoruba people from wrongdoing and promote social order.

Under the direction of male and female Gelede society officials, the mask carvers, costume preparers, music and song writers, choreographers, singers, drummers, and dancers are organized to perform. All are men, with the occasional exception of female singers. Gelede is usually held during the dry season from March to May, as well as at funerals of important leaders and community celebrations. Gelede is held in the community's marketplace, the women's center of activities.

Although any human activity could be the theme of Gelede since hardly anything could exist without "our mothers," three themes dominate—to recognize and promote positive, productive activities; to ridicule and discourage negative, destructive activities; and to communicate the traditional beliefs and thoughts of the group.

The theme of a Gelede performance is expressed through masked dances and songs. The dancers' specific sequential movements are called *eka* and are carefully choreographed to drum rhythms. Although all the masqueraders are men, they always appear in pairs, with one assuming a male role and the other a female role. This paired masquerade indicates that the complementarity of the sexes is fundamental to the totality of the universe.

Depending on the specific theme, Gelede masks can take a variety of forms, including human beings, animals, inanimate objects, or any combination of these elements. The masks represent various occupations, activities, metaphors, and spirits, and may express overlapping meanings. Each headdress is carved out of a single block of wood. Some have elaborate superstructures that are attached using a variety of joints on top of the helmet. Many of these headdresses are colored with polychrome paints and exhibit the artists' innovativeness and

virtuosity, as well as the Yoruba aesthetic tradition. Ketu Kingdom, now a city state in the western Yorubaland, is considered to have originated Gelede sometime during its expansion in the late eighteenth century after the Ketu had migrated from the ancient kingdom of Oyo. The Ketu were known for a rich cultural tradition and skillful wood-carving.

This fine example may have been carved by an artist from the Ketu area. The simple coiffure and the three broad, bold-lined scarifications on the cheeks and forehead suggest that it represents a person of high spirituality and *ase*, or life force. Her bulging eyes signify a spiritually charged state, and the dyed head signifies possession of a "deep knowledge of *Ifa*" (verses of ancient Yoruba thought).   CTM

28 INNER HOUSE OF THE HEAD (IBORI)

Yoruba, Nigeria
Fabric, glass beads,
cowrie shells
h. 19.1 cm (7¹/₂ in.)
Collection of
Samuel Thomas, Jr.

The Yoruba of southwestern Nigeria consider the human head (*ori*) to be the point of exit and entry of spirits to the being. As such, the head is the object of much ritual attention. In religious circles, the preparation of the head is essential for a devotee to be possessed by a deity. A typical Yoruba family would inquire through divination about the head of its newborn before the child is given a name. It is at such rituals that close relatives learn of the taboos, totems, potentials, and otherworldly associations of the child. The child's spiritual and material well-being depends on strict adherence to the prescriptions of the diviner given at birth, and the family would protect this vital information. As a result of these well-known spiritual and social associations, the human head receives substantial emphasis in Yoruba art, often making up about a third or quarter of the sculpted human form.

This relatively abstract object is another of the head's multiple manifestations with complex philosophical underpinnings. Referred to as an *ibori*, the piece constitutes the core of an elaborate artistic construction known as *ile ori* or literally, "house of the head." Yoruba beliefs about the ibori are tied to notions of individual survival and well-being. At the center of this belief is the view that the head can influence human destiny.

Yoruba religion distinguishes between an inner and outer head, with the former taking precedence over the latter. The inner head is the locus of the vital force (*ase*) that resides in everyone, a quality that defines individuality (Drewal et al. 1989). The ile ori and its related ibori form a complex, two-part assemblage. The ile ori, a cylindrical cloth and leather construction topped with a cone and decorated with cowrie shells, is the outer shell. The ibori, totally enveloped in the ile ori, is the actual receptacle into which sacred elements—a child's placenta and ancestral or cult materials—are placed. These are elements of kinship with religious significance. The security of the ibori's contents are intimately linked to the capacity of its owner to succeed.

Although the ibori's shape may be similar to that of the ile ori, it is frequently more abstract. The stem that projects from its top terminates in a medicinal bulb designed to link the head with the heavens (*orun*) and to protect its sacred contents. The cowries are a reference to both achievement and the potential to prosper. Together with the multicolored glass beads, the materials reflect the owner's pedigree, wealth, and prestige. Overlapping cowries are said to imitate the white feathers of the bird of wisdom, reinforcing the Yoruba association of the human head with judgment and material success (Thompson 1983, 46).

Conical forms are pervasive in Yoruba sacred art, ranging from simple mounds that guard entrances to the elaborately bead-embroidered crowns of divine kings. Indeed, the ibori's shape recalls the form of the Yoruba royal crown with its vertical protuberance and four side flaps. Such "projections from the top" have been variously interpreted as alluding to an inherent potent spiritual force; a protective presence; and a "visual command," symbolizing the contact between the ibori's contents and the upper universe, *orun*, or realm of spirits (M. Drewal 1977; H. Drewal 1977).   NQ

Provenance: Peter Boyd, Seattle, Washington

29 MALE FIGURE

Tabwa, Zaire

Wood

h. 37.2 cm (14⁵/₈ in.)

Faxon Collection

The Tabwa are from the southeastern part of Zaire where northern Zambia meets Tanzania. Traditionally, Tabwa carved wooden figures such as this one represent ancestors and occasionally earth spirits, who are adept at healing. These figures, collectively known as *mikisi*, were housed and cared for by the elders of specific families in special buildings within residential compounds. Family members would go to these buildings to communicate with the spirits inherent in the figures, which they believed had the power to protect and heal. For the same reasons, the figures might also be placed at crucial points in the village to keep evil forces from disrupting the activities of the community.

This example is unusual in that it lacks body scarification and the arms are straight at the sides rather than bent at the elbow. The dark encrusted patination on the figure's head suggests that it may have been used ceremonially and received sacrifices.   MK

Provenance: Harvey Menist, Amsterdam

SYMBOLS OF PASSAGE

TRANSITIONS IN HUMAN LIFE—birth, puberty, marriage, and death—are significant in many African cultures, for they represent experiences that usher in a new phase of social existence. At the same time, these changes place the effected individuals in a state of grave spiritual danger. The risks associated with these passages are believed to be enormous. Consequently, while practices differ from culture to culture, diverse rituals and art mark these occasions to alleviate fears and to facilitate orderly transitions.

There is no doubt that such rites of passage have benefits for both individuals and the community. The timing and orchestration of coming-of-age ceremonies, for example, represents a strategy that enables the older generation to phase itself into a secondary position while passing authority on to the young. The symbolism bestows privileges and rights to the new adults along with imposing tremendous responsibilities. Through the instructional agenda of a funeral or initiation performance, a solemn ritual becomes an important educational experience with the music, dances, and recited verses reinforcing ancestral norms. Successful completion of these periodic formalities assure the solidarity of the group, as mutual recognition and respect among its segments are reaffirmed and the souls of its departed are mobilized for the benefit of society.

In the majority of groups in Africa, art objects play a substantial role in insuring success in transitional rites. Many visual forms may be featured with carved masks and figures making up the largest number of images. These objects perform critical functions, enhancing the meaning of each passage. For birth in particular, there are artistic types created solely to alleviate female infertility, to insure safe delivery, or to capture symbolically the essence of birth itself.

However, it is aesthetic forms connected with puberty rites, including circumcisions and initiation, that dominate. Commonly the young boys and girls coming of age are placed in "bush schools" in secluded locations, frequently outside the community. For a child to attain his or her new adult status, he or she must symbolically die and be reborn. The contact between the initiate and the work of art may be to instruct or to pass along knowledge as in the case of the Bamana *chi wara*, which accomplishes this goal through performances.

A wide array of roles tend to be assigned to art objects. Some visual forms are employed in policing or protecting the young initiates from spiritual dangers, such as in the case of the *sowei* masquerades of the Mende of Sierra Leone. Others perform purely symbolic functions: for instance, the painted bodily decorations and temporary adornment with sacred priestly straw hats convey the beauty and purity of Krobo Dipo initiates during final ceremonies that mark their achievement of womanhood. Incidentally, it is this public display that sets them up for marriage as prospective suitors get to see them in full splendor.

Funerary rites, to a great extent, center around African concerns with the consequences of death, for even though the mortal remains may perish, the spirit survives. Apprehension over

what happens in the hereafter, particularly the destiny of the soul and its ability to influence life among the living, underpins elaborate ceremonies and protocols designed to guarantee smooth passage to the spirit world. For most African peoples, the afterlife generally mirrors the living community. Social status and political rank can therefore be replicated in the spirit realm; hence the tendency for the Akan royalty to be buried with gold emblems of their political authority to enable them to transfer their distinct statuses to the next life.

Young female adults being welcomed by the community at the Payem festival after completing the Dipo initiation ritual. Shai, Ghana 1988.

A variety of works, frequently sculpted portraits of the deceased, may be part of the actual burial or funeral of well-to-do people. Rendered in a non-perishable medium such as terracotta or bronze, these forms may represent the dead only in a general sense. They may be viewed as actual surrogates for the deceased and thus be accorded enormous respect. Funerary figures, such as those of the Akan and Benin peoples, become the centerpieces of altars or shrines dedicated to the memory of the dead, sometimes serving as receptacles for the soul.

In addition to these idealized images of ancestors, some African societies may choose to memorialize their collective dead through elaborate public ritual, such as the Akan *adae* ceremony held every forty days, or through masquerades such as the Yoruba *egungun*. Festivals held following a funeral are designed to recognize the importance of the dead to the life of the community, particularly to reinforce their contributions to economic well-being and spiritual protection. These performances complement the efficacy of the works of art used in them.   NQ

30 MASK (OKUKWÉ)

Galoa, Gabon
Wood, white and black
paint, raffia
h. 25.4 cm (10 in.)
Private Collection

The Galoa inhabit the lake regions of the middle Ogowe River basin in western Gabon. Now mixed with the southernmost Fang and other Omyènè peoples of the Ogowe delta, their traditional culture has largely disappeared, and like most Gabonese, the Galoa are predominantly Christian. Masks are exceedingly rare, and little is known of their original meanings and uses.

The few published examples are all, like this piece, *Okukwé* masks, sharing the concave face, narrow-slit eyes, and distinctive triangular black decoration on the forehead and chin. Although they fall within the geographic boundaries of the famous "white masks of the Ogowe," Galoa masks differ from the better known Mitsogho, Punu, and Vuvi examples in their symbolic use of color. In an unexplained inversion, the Galoa perceive white as a beneficent color, while black is associated with death, war, and aggression (Perrois 1979, 237).

The general term for Galoa masked figures is *okouyi,* but only initiated men were permitted to use this name. Women, children, and strangers referred to the figures with the respectful title "great chief" or "great man." Each spirit who manifested itself through a figure also had a specific name, which it shared with the mask (Perrois 1979, 237). Galoa masks appeared

during funeral rites, at celebrations of the birth of twins, at the return of an important village member after a prolonged absence, and during the initiation rites of young men (Perrois 1979, 237). The masks were thus associated with all aspects of village life from birth to death, which may explain the prominent juxtaposition of black and white on both the mask and its raffia costume.

Okukwé masks were sometimes painted black and used by members of a judiciary society to help discover the sorcerers responsible for sudden deaths, accidents, or illnesses in the village (Perrois 1979, 47). They could also function more generally as enforcers of social order, shaming wrongdoers into proper behavior by publicly disclosing their actions (Perrois 1986a, 99-100).   PM

Provenance: Reynold Kerr, New York

③ MASK (*LUKWAKONGO*)

Lega, Zaire
Wood, kaolin
h. 20.3 x 19.7 cm
(8 x 7 3/4 in.)
The Collection of Dede
and Oscar Feldman

The Bwami association is a cohesive social force that is central to Lega society, art, and religion. Membership in Bwami transcends kinship and lineage; all circumcised males and their wives are eligible to join the association, which has five grades, or levels, for men and three complementary ones for women. Initiation to each grade is based on a sequence of rites that preserve intellectual, moral, social, and economic standards in the community.

Sculpture is an integral part of Bwami ideology. Masks function as tools for acquiring spiritual knowledge and serve as insignia of rank. Most initiation objects are used at different grade levels, and objects have no single symbolic meaning (Biebuyck 1986, 25). This small wooden mask is known as *lukwakongo,* a type made specifically for the *yananio* grade, the second highest level of membership in the association. They are primarily owned by members of the *lutumbo lwa yananio,* the highest of two divisions in the yananio grade.

These masks are used in the two- or three-day initiation ceremonies of lutumbo lwa yananio to dramatize Lega proverbs and to facilitate the incarnation of a number of legendary ancestors. The Bwami view the masks, often referred to as skulls, as embodiments of their ancestors. The mask is part of a cyclical transference of values between the living and the dead and serves as a visual reminder of the teachings established by the forbearers. When a member dies, his symbols of rank are temporarily displayed at his grave. After the funerary ceremonies, the mask is transferred to the next initiate as a symbol of his status.

Lukwakongo are used in several rites of the lutumbo lwa yananio, and an initiate must bring the symbols of his rank to the ceremonies he attends. Masks may be used singularly or with a group of other objects. The range of meanings and practices associated with these masks vary from each community. Whatever the purpose, the ritual maintains common elements that include dramatic performances, presentation of the initiate, interpretation of proverbs, the transfer of insignia, and distributions of food, gifts, and payments (Biebuyck 1985, 16, 141).

This mask illustrates the formal conventions of the lukwakongo type, which are usually round or oval in shape. They often have fiber beards made of raffia or banana tree bark, which refer to the ancestors. A red or brown patina is achieved through the application of oils and camwood pigment. The small facial plane is typically heart-shaped and set off by white clay or kaolin. Ornamental designs include small holes arranged on the forehead resembling tattoo patterns (Biebuyck 1985, 129).

Masks may be carried; tied to the knees or the front or the back of the head; held under the chin; swung in the air, or dragged on the ground. They are sometimes placed on a fence or laid out on the ground as a reference to the authority of the ancestors during warfare. It has been suggested that during times of war the Lega warriors would rub white clay around the eyes and nose, and this practice may have influenced Bwami mask production (Biebuyck 1994, 190).   MLW

Provenance: Marc Felix, Brussels

㉜ FEMALE FIGURE (NYELENI)

Bamana, Mali

Wood, brass tacks

h. 48.9 cm (19¹/₄ in.)

Anonymous Loan

The Bamana are the largest ethnic group in the Republic of Mali, inhabiting the triangular region in the southwestern portion of the country, the southernmost point of which borders on the Côte d'Ivoire. This figure comes from the southern Bamana area and is most likely associated with the Jo association, a hierarchical society that teaches proper modes of social behavior and also helps to shape the political and spiritual lives of its members.

The Jo association is one of two secret societies in the southern Bamana area, the other being the Gwan society, both of which are unique in Bamana culture in that they allow both male and female initiates. Ethnographic documentation of these associations is relatively meager, largely due to the fact that the initiation ceremonies employing figural sculpture are performed only once every seven years. In addition, participation in these ceremonies has sharply declined since the late 1970s with the conversion of many Bamana people to Islam (Ezra 1983, iv; 1986, 15).

In villages participating in the Jo society, membership is mandatory for all Bamana boys, but it is not uncommon for young women to be separately initiated to the early stages of membership (Ezra 1983, 58). Young men may rise through the ranks with each seven-year initiation ceremony, acquiring esoteric knowledge as well as the responsibilities that come with it. There are a multitude of subdivisions with varying rituals, instruments, costumes, and sculpture in the complex association structure.

After circumcision and an intense six-year period for learning about Jo, initiates undergo symbolic deaths and are reborn as children of Joö during a week long initiation retreat. Upon returning to the village, the young initiates are divided into groups to celebrate their new status and display their knowledge by performing the new songs and dances they learned. The first performance is for their home villages, while the next several months are spent touring neighboring communities where they receive food, cotton, and money for their entertainment (Ezra 1986, 16).

It is the performing blacksmith group, *numu jo*, that uses figurative sculpture similar to this one in its initiation performances. Jo association figures always depict women, usually standing on a small circular base and with a saggital crest on top of the head. The high crest down the center of the head is part of a coiffure worn by both men and women, which is usually embellished by hanging locks of hair on the sides of the head. The style of these coiffures varies from figure to figure and is sometimes covered by a high hat, leaving only the locks exposed. Even when worn by women, the hat is generally believed to represent that of the male hunters' association or the hunters' bards society, which are said to possess great knowledge and supernatural powers. A female figure depicted with one of these hats indicates that she embodies the same attributes of power (Ezra 1983, 147-49).

During performances, the figures are either held by the dancing initiates or placed in the area of the entertainment (Imperato 1983, 39). These carved figures act as representations of the ideal physical attributes of young women available for marriage (Ezra 1988, 17, 18). The flattened upper body with broad shoulders and protruding conical breasts, the slender cylindrical torso with slightly swollen abdomen, and the full, exaggerated buttocks are all distinctive features of the nyeleni and refer to Bamana ideals of feminine beauty and fertility. The sculptures are called *joyeleni*, or more commonly *nyeleni*, meaning "pretty little one" or "little ornament," a name traditionally given to firstborn daughters.

Prior to the performance, these sculptures are shined with oil to make them more alluring, much as a young Bamana woman might do to prepare herself for a dance ceremony (Ezra 1988, 18). In addition, the figures are clothed and embellished with jewelry in the fashion of a young unmarried woman, and the decorative pattern of incised lines on the torso, common in Jo figurative sculpture, may refer to scarification marks sometimes displayed by Bamana girls (Ezra 1988, 21). Despite a vow of celibacy by the initiates during these performances, one of the purposes of the ceremonies is for the young men to find marriage partners. The sculptures may then be used to promote the institution of marriage as the young initiates complete their rite of passage (McNaughton 1995, 500).   TS

Provenance: Pace Gallery, New York

33 HORSE HEAD

Bamana, Mali
Wood
38.7 x 12.7 cm
(15¹/₄ x 5 in.)
The Collection of Charles,
Gail, and Lyndsay McGee

This horse head probably is related to the Jo association of the southern Bamana, where such sculptural figures are known to be used in ceremonies of one of the society's many subgroups, *bû*, the "masters of the horse." Although used in both religious and secular ceremonies, the figures have until recently been identified simply as horse or mule heads, with little knowledge of their function (Ezra 1983, 103, 105, 106).

In the ceremonies of this group, these horse heads are attached to simple wooden bodies and ridden by members during traveling performances that celebrate their initiation into the Jo society. In contrast to the elegantly carved head, the body is made up of a sticklike torso inserted into the hollow area of the neck and fastened through holes on either side. Legs similarly are composed of wooden rods inserted into the thin body. The frame is then wrapped with fibers to create a weighty appearance. Although the elaborate heads are fairly common in Western collections, it is extremely rare to find the body armatures outside of their indigenous environments (Ezra 1983, 103).

While the horse functions as a unified entity during Jo initiation ceremonies, it is only the head that receives decoration. This may be because, in much African art, the head is the most important element of the figure. The black glossy surface and the incised zigzag and band patterns on the face are characteristic attributes of Mande craftsmanship. The circular indentations on the sides of the muzzle may have been used to hold pieces of mirrors, and the perforations at the top of the ears probably once held strands of red and white fana seeds, beads, or cowries, which are often used to signify wealth and status. The young initiates who ride these horses perform warlike dances, dressed in black-dyed shirts and skirts and brandishing wooden lances (Ezra 1983, 103-05).   TS

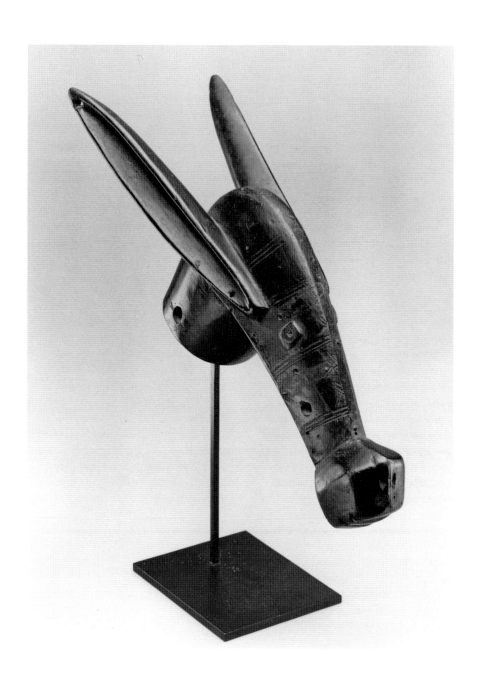

through the embodiment of a Bundu spirit associated with a water deity. Sowo are commissioned solely by Bundu officials within the parameters of a long established specifications.

The carver is always male. He must respect the secrecy of Bundu society and possess the skills needed to create a mask that possesses the high aesthetic standard needed in the Bundu tradition. In addition, he must make the mask as light and comfortable as possible in order for the wearer to dance well, a crucial quality for an ideal woman. The masks are carved no thicker than three-quarter inches, have a smooth and delicate interior, provide sufficient visibility through the eye openings, and are balanced and steady on the shoulders. To obtain a clean, shiny surface, like that of a well-groomed Sande woman, the artist smooths the mask with rough leaves, dyes it black with repeated applications of plant substances, and polishes it with palm oil.

This example exhibits the desired physical qualities of Bundu women with regional characteristics attributed to the Vai or Gola peoples on the border of Sierra Leone and Liberia. The overall shape and design are symmetrical and harmonious. The forehead, said to project one's personality, is abundant and round, a symbol of honesty, success, and power. The neatly styled coiffure indicates orderliness; ungroomed hair signifies insanity. The elaborate superstructure may contain elements that have proverbial significance. The closed eyes are essential, for direct eye contact is considered disrespectful. The ears are carefully shaped since the ability to hear is believed never to die. The small closed mouth signifies the spiritual power of silence. The neck folds, rendered on most Mende masks, may represent the fat rings of prosperity or water ripples associated with the legend that the original sowo mask came out of the water—a symbolic image of rebirth.   CTM

Provenance: Collection of Almamy Diabi, Ambassador from Guinea

34 **BUNDU SOCIETY HELMET MASK (SOWO)**

Mende, Sierra Leone
Wood, raffia
41.9 x 21.6 cm
(16 1/2 x 8 1/2 in.)
Collection of Dr. Sarah Carolyn Adams Reese

Bundu is a secret society exclusively for women; women have governed, administered, and participated in it for more than five hundred years. Across Sierra Leone, women are united, regardless of their nationality, ethnicity, wealth, or status, through memberships in numerous local chapters of the Bundu society. The Bundu is a prerequisite for an adult woman. A girl remains a child unless she endures the fear and pain of Bundu initiation, which transforms her, both physically and mentally, by circumcision and strict discipline. Bundu is a hierarchical institution headed by a *sowei*, the highest ranking female in society. Educational, political, social, religious, and artistic activities are offered during the dry winter season. The group provides a shelter for women, teaching them skills and the strength to survive hardships in a community in which female members of a family are greatly responsible for farming. Women share a dwelling separate from male family members.

The masks for the Bundu society are called *sowo*, and unlike other masks in Africa, they can only be worn by women. These masks embody "the visual representation and compilation of aspirations and ideals for womanhood" (Boone, 1986, 39). These qualities are demonstrated by the sowei and passed down for generations with respect and admiration. The masks also symbolize the ethical principles, harmony, and justice associated with Bundu authority. A British commissioner who witnessed Bundu practices at the beginning of this century recorded that sowo masks appeared in dancing associated with the initiation rites and also served to police any violators who approached the secret Bundu bush school. The masks' authority is established

MASK

Bassa, Liberia
Wood, white pigment
l. 26.7 cm (10½ in.)
Faxon Collection

While most African masks are placed either vertically over the face, horizontally on top of the head, or completely cover the head like a helmet, this crescent-moon shaped Bassa mask is worn in a particular way all its own. The Bassa mask is attached to a cap on the forehead and worn with a costume consisting of a cloth top and voluminous raffia skirt. The unique way in which the mask is worn accounts for its sharply curved shape, which allows for unperforated eyes. These features distinguish Bassa masks from the better-known ones of the Dan in northwestern Liberia.

The Bassa produce two general types of masks: ritual ones associated with initiations and portrait masks, such as this example. The ritual masks have a fierce appearance, combining both zoomorphic and anthropomorphic features, and represent a Bassa for-

est spirit. Portrait masks are not supposed to exhibit the likeness of any individual ancestor but rather they are "conceived and carved according to tribal sculptural laws transmitted through generations of masters" (Meneghini 1972, 47) to create a peaceful appearance in accordance with Bassa definitions of beauty. They represent ancestral spirits believed to protect the community. Another type of portrait mask embodies devils and is worn by entertainers "at festivals as an agent of social control" (Meneghini 1972, 47). There are also miniature portrait masks carried by individuals in order to privately communicate with the ancestor represented by the mask.

The neatly lobed hair style, large round forehead, half opened eyes, straight nose, carefully shaped ears, and small mouth and chin are all elements of the Bassa ideal of female beauty. The mask's characteristic deep dark surfaces were achieved through time-consuming applications of leaf extracts. Traces of white chalk are visible around the eyes and forehead, and the white dots on the cheeks may originally have been multicolored.   CTM

36 HEADDRESS (CHI WARA)

Bamana, Mali
Wood
22.9 x 15.2 cm
(9 x 6 in.)
Private Collection

This headdress is used in dance rituals that recall Chi Wara, the spirit who introduced agriculture to the Bamana of Mali. According to legend, the half-animal and half-man Chi Wara tilled the ground using his claws and a wooden stick. He grew corn and millet in a field where there had only previously been weeds and taught other men to do the same. A man who becomes a good farmer may be referred to as Chi Wara, which is also the name of an initiation society for men.

Chi wara headdresses often depict the curved horns of the roan antelope or the straight horns of the oryx, but the abstract form of this example more closely resembles the arched back of the pangolin. The shape of the pangolin has been likened to "the tension of muscles needed for the hard labor of hand-hoe agriculture," making the animal a symbol for those qualities necessary for a man to be a good farmer: durability, strength, and persistance (Roberts 1995, 83).

The cross-hatched markings, which appear over the entire surface of the headdress, recall the plated, armor-like scales of the pangolin. These marks are also evidence of the historical and cultural connections of the Bamana and the nearby Mande cultures of the Western Sudan. As the chi wara ritual performances are used to instruct the Bamana in community values and culture, the Mande "often use animals in metaphors that comment upon social life and the human condition" (McNaughton 1995, 502).

In Bamana society, those who sculpt the headdresses belong to a blacksmith caste called *numu*. The choice of style was generally left up to the carver, although sometimes a particular form, perhaps imitating a well-liked headdress from another village, was requested (Imperato 1970, 74). The face is not readily evident on this headdress; it is depicted by small angular cuts marking the forehead, eyes, nose, and mouth. Small holes found along the curving arch of the headdress probably once held rings and beads to further adorn the sculpture. The larger holes in the base of the chi wara were used to attach the headdress to a basket cap worn on the top of the dancer's head. The dancer also wore a costume of raffia and woven fibers of the *da* plant to cover his face and body.

The individual who dances the chi wara is not chosen because he is necessarily the best farmer but because he is the best dancer in the community. Nevertheless, the best farmer is often recognized in the ritual performance. According to one account, he wears a costume essentially the same as that of chi wara, except that the headdress is of a smaller size (Imperato 1970, 76). For this reason, it may be argued that the Detroit sculpture was actually worn by a champion farmer.   ON

Provenance: Malcolm Franklin, San Francisco, California; Merton Simpson, New York; Donald Morris Gallery, Birmingham, Michigan

 APE MASK (SO'O)

Hemba, Zaire

Wood

h. 20.3 cm (8 in.)

Private Collection

Among the Hemba of Zaire, funerals are the most important cultural activity and may last from several days to weeks or months, depending upon the age and complexity of the deceased's social standing. Following a period of intense mourning, which is characterized by sleeping outdoors and otherwise abstaining from normal activities, the funerary rites culminate in the important *ubuzha malilo* festival. It is at this time that inheritance disputes and the assignment of responsibility for the death are determined (Blakely and Blakely 1987, 34). In Hemba thinking, death is always perceived as ultimately caused through human agency, whether intentional or not, and the assessment of guilt and exaction of restitution are essential for greater social healing.

It is in the context of this culminating funerary festival that the *so'o,* or "chimpanzee-human," masquerade is performed. The mask and costume combine animal and human features to create a grotesque figure, whose confusion of civilized and wild elements are deeply disturbing. The wide-open mouth, never interpreted as smiling, is the most salient characteristic of its simian identification, as it contrasts sharply with the Hemba practice of maintaining closed-mouth dignity. Also important in this regard are the sharply raised eyebrows, indicating a stare associated with drunkenness and insanity. The physical similarity with chimpanzees is heightened by the attachment of fur pelts to the costume, which underscores the connection with the untamed forest, as does the noise created by the attachment of iron bells to create a high-pitched squeal evocative of simian vocalizations (Blakely and Blakely 1987, 32-34).

The Hemba view chimpanzees with trepidation, as they are perceived as fiercely predatory. At the first of the so'o's two appearances, the typical reaction is fear. The masquerader initially chases spectators (particularly women and children), who are forced to flee to the safety of a cultivated field, which the masked spirit will never enter. In this phase of the performance, the Hemba never stare at the masquerade, and if captured by it are forced to undergo initiation into the so'o society (Blakely and Blakely 1987, 35). Initiation is also warranted for a woman whose child is born with its eyes closed, and in the event of prolonged crop failure (Blakely and Blakely 1987, 33-34). These conditions suggest an important link to fertility and fecundity, which creates an interesting duality with the death associations of the masquerade.

The second appearance of the so'o at the funeral festival is markedly different from the first. The aggressive chasing is replaced by lighthearted dancing. The audience is now free to watch the performance, encircling the figure and sometimes joining in the dance. The amusement and happiness generated in the funerary context are important symbols of the return to normal social behaviors after the intense period of mourning.

Overall, then, the so'o masquerade seems to reflect the ambivalence of death. By combining human and animal features, and thus crossing the boundaries that normally separate them, the chimpanzee-human is a liminal figure paralleling the status of the newly deceased as neither living nor ancestral. The wildness of the masks disrupts normal social behavior in the same manner as death, crossing social and spatial boundaries (Blakely and Blakely 1987, 36). PM

Provenance: Marc Felix, Brussels

38 MASK (KIBWABWABWA)

Mbagani (Babindji), Zaire

Wood, kaolin

h. 34.9 cm (13 ³/₄ in.)

Private Collection

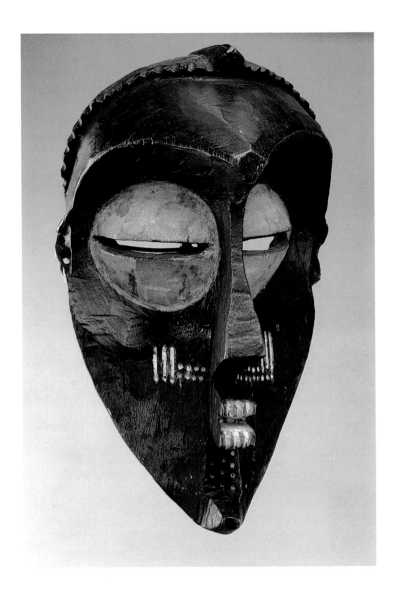

The Mbagani reside in the borderlands of Zaire and Angola. While the Mbagani share certain cultural features with neighboring groups, little is known of their history or art. The most commonly published Mbagani pieces are the *kibwabwabwa* masks, characterized by a sharply pointed chin and oversized, whitened eye sockets. As in this example, the eye openings are usually depicted as narrow slits, with the lips rendered in parallel rectangular forms. A cord passed through the small hole beneath the nose would have been clenched between the wearer's teeth, holding the mask securely during a performance. These facial characteristics are also found on certain masks of the Lwalwa, Bena Lulua, and southern Kete peoples, although none of these neighboring groups emphasize the eyes as dramatically as do the Mbagani, nor is the head as emphatically crescent-shaped. The vertical lines on either side of the nose probably represent scarification or facial painting, and may be indicative of the widespread Chokwe cultural influence in this region.

Although the kibwabwabwa has generally been assumed to function in the circumcision rites of adolescent boys, more recently it has been suggested that the mask may also be associated with the *mukanda* society. The mukanda institution is found among many Zairian peoples (Herreman and Petridis 1993, 106). Its members collectively supervise the mundane aspects of village life, while the village chief presides over more important governmental issues. However, during such crisis periods as widespread crop failure, infertility, or unsuccessful hunts, the mukanda assumes a more powerful role. It is during these times that this mask performs, accompanied by both a masked and unmasked figure.

Presumably their appearance serves to placate the offended spirits and ancestors whose wrath is perceived as responsible for misfortune (Ceyssens 1993, in Herreman and Petridis 1993, 97).

Among the Chokwe and several other ethnic groups, it is the mukanda association that is responsible for the circumcision of young men (Consentino 1982, 209). During the period of their seclusion in the bush, the initiates learn important social mores and fashion their own masks from bark cloth and fibers, and they dance them on their return to the village. It is unclear however, whether the Mbagani association performs a similar function. The presence of kaolin around the eye sockets of kibwabwabwa masks suggests its use in initiatory contexts. In many Zairian cultures, white clay is applied to the faces and bodies of persons undergoing rites of passage or initiation, situations that are perceived as liminal and thus spiritually dangerous. In addition,

kaolin is symbolic of the ritually purified state necessary for successful communication with the spiritual and ancestral realms. These dual uses of kaolin suggest that the *kibwabwabwa* may fulfill multiple roles in Mbagani culture. In this regard, it is noteworthy that the masks of the neighboring Lwalwa peoples are used in both circumcision rites and times of poor hunting (Timmermans 1967, 82, 85).   PM

Provenance: H. Kerels, Belgium; Jef van der Straete, Belgium; Merton Simpson, New York; Donald Morris, Birmingham, Michigan

39 HELMET MASK (HEMBE OR GEEMBA)

Suku, Zaire

Wood, pigment, raffia

45.7 x 38.1 cm

(18 x 15 in.)

Anonymous Lender

Hembe masks such as this piece appear at the end of the Sukunda initiation rites of manhood, *mukanda*, signaling the end of the young males' rigorous training period, which is intended to increase their endurance and moral integrity. The presence of masked dancers at the end of the rite marks the candidates' "coming-out" into manhood. On this occasion, masking provides the initiates with the opportunity to ceremoniously affirm their new status in the community.

The hembe mask possesses an intrinsic power that cures and protects the participants of mukanda, perhaps because of its power to ward off danger (Bourgeois 1979, 77; Biebuyck 1985, 208). Prior to initiation rites, the masks are anointed with a substance made of animal bone, snake heads, insects, and the blood of a rooster, which activates the mask as a charm (Bourgeois 1981, 32). Additional magical substances are placed inside the mask or underneath the raffia collar to target witches who might want to harm the dancer in his task of leading young males into adulthood. The mask is consequently used with great care after much instruction. Unsanctioned handling could cause harm.

The hembe, a bell-shaped helmet mask, is distinctive among the northern Suku, although not exclusive to them. The masks are worn in male/female pairs. The male masks have zoomorphic images of the horned antelope, monkeys, serpents or birds, connected to proverbs and hunting, while the female ones display an elaborate crested coiffure. The piece illustrated here is a female mask.   MLW

Provenance: Marc Felix, Brussels

40 MASK
above **(MBUYA MBANGU)**

Pende (central/western)
Zaire
Wood, white and black
pigment, raffia
h. 22.9 cm (9 in.)
Florence and
Donald Morris

41 MASK
opposite **(PANYA NGOMBE)**

Pende (eastern), Zaire
Wood, red, white,
and black pigment
55.9 x 26.7 cm
(22 x 10 ¹/₂ in.)
Private Collection

These two masks represent the traditions of the principal Pende groups. Originally from western Angola, today the Pende inhabit a large area of southeastern Zaire. As a result of several migrations during the eighteenth and nineteenth centuries, the Pende were split into several groups, often referred to as eastern and western Pende.

Politically, the Pende are organized into numerous independent chiefdoms comprising various clans and lineages. The chief, an honorary and religious title, is considered the giver of life. He presides over planting and harvesting and is thought to be an intermediary with ancestors. All Pende chiefs and lineage heads have a ritual house built especially for them. The ritual house, associated with the survival of the village, its people, and the surrounding environment, is used to store the royal treasure, or *kifumu,* and other insignia of chiefly power and authority.

Typically, the architectural plan of the house consists of a small doorway or vestibule, two rooms, and a courtyard surrounded and concealed by stakes. Entry into the architectural structure is restricted. Only the chief's minister, who performs the most important rituals, is permitted to enter the inner chamber containing the chief's coffin, special medicines used to protect the chief, and the three "masks of chiefly insignia" (Strother 1993, 165). One of these masks is known as the *panya ngombe.*

Elaborately decorated ritual houses, called *kibulu,* are found among the eastern Pende. The domed rooftops are decorated with sculpture of animals and human figures while the doorways are adorned with carved, polychromed panels. Above the entrance hangs an incised lintel or large, wooden mask, based upon the *panya ngombe* mask. The use of this type of mask as a lintel is reserved for only the highest ranking chiefs.

It signifies the prestige and status of a chief who has the right to commence initiations into the men's society, an elaborate ceremony that is held every ten to twenty years (Biebuyck 1985, 223).

The mask itself is believed to represent the bushcow or buffalo. Worn by a dancer dressed in chief's attire and carrying a machete, the masquerader performs during ceremonies initiating adolescent boys into adulthood. During the closing activities of the initiation ceremony, the *panya ngombe* mask circulates through the village collecting offerings and tribute from subordinate chiefs and the initiates' fathers.

Among the central and western Pende, wooden masks called *mbuya*, were formerly of importance to the different festivities surrounding circumsion and initiation rites. They have also been linked with hunting, planting, and healing rituals. They were carved in what is referred to as the "Katundu" style and usually represent specific character types such as the clown, sorcerer, prostitute, and chief.

This example, referred to as *mbuya mbangu*, is one of three masks that portray "villainous or ugly persons". The mask is colored half black and half white and has facial distortions, such as the vertically positioned mouth and bent nose. The visual duality of the contrasting paint stems from general beliefs about opposing forces of good and evil, sickness and health. Mbangu is often described as an epileptic who fell into a fire causing half of his face to be burned. Other descriptions suggest that the mask depicts someone who has been bewitched and thus suffers from facial paralysis or other physical disabilities and personal misfortune (Biebuyck 1985, 240). The mbangu masker also is identified by his humpback. He usually has either an arrow in the hump or carrys bows and arrows, a reference to "shooting" one's prey by casting a spell. Additional paraphernalia worn by the dancer may include wooden bells, like those typically used on hunting dogs. Metaphorically, the mbangu reflects the Pende belief that illness and misfortune, often the result of malice from others, can strike anyone at any moment. Therefore, one should not mock or laugh at those afflicted but extend support (Biebuyck 1985, 240; Cornet 1978, 127; Strother 1995, 314).   LR

Provenance:
41. Charles Fox, San Francisco, California

43 MASK (GOLI)

below Baule, Côte d'Ivoire
Wood
40.6 x 22.9 cm
(16 in. x 9 in.)
The Collection of Dede
and Oscar Feldman

This wooden mask is part of the *goli* dance performance designed to entertain in a variety of contexts, particularly funerals and rites to honor the dead, agricultural harvests, and visits of notables to the community.

Baule *goli* masks depict a range of subjects, including animals and distinguished people, as well as a wide spectrum of characters—a slave or a prostitute, for example—found in a typical Baule community. The costume of the masker usually comprises a raffia and cloth outfit together with headgear made of an animal skin. In performance, each mask comes out in order of its importance, first the bestial and then the human forms. Those masks intended as portraits of renowned persons in the community play an honorific role, sometimes dancing alongside the individuals they depict. Some masks are also danced in male-female pairs (Vogel 1977, 1981).

Historically, the goli has much stronger roots among the Wan, Mande-speaking neighbors of the Baule. The Baule evidently borrowed this entertainment from the Wan (Roy 1992, 62), although it is doubtful the mask originated with the Wan, since strikingly similar face masks have been documented among other Mande-related peoples such as the Guro and the Senufo. The Senufo *kpeli-yehe* and Guro *zamle* masks, like Baule goli forms, have elaborately carved coiffures but rarely feature animal headdresses. Because both polished and painted face masks are produced and used by the Baule, it is possible the Baule are influenced by styles from all these other groups. What is perhaps exclusively Baule, however, is the tendency toward fleshier and more voluptuous forms, as well as the distinctive keloidal scars on the forehead and beneath the eyes.   NQ

Provenance: Alain de Mon Brison, Paris

42 MASK

above Kete, Zaire
Wood, raffia
h. 50.8 cm (20 in.)
Faxon Collection

The Kete are an agricultural people residing along the southern border of the Kuba Bushong kingdom, who have historically been tributaries of the Kuba kings. Like other vassals of the Kuba, the Kete's contribution to the dominant Kuba culture is unclear; however, Kuba oral history credits the Kete for their masking traditions.

A broad group of masks have been associated with Kete initiation rites, while a considerable number are reserved for funerals of important personages. This Kete mask belongs to the latter category. The mask bears a striking resemblance to the Kuba *mboom* or *bwoom* image, reinforcing the assertion that the Kuba may have borrowed artistic styles from their Kete subjects. There are many intriguing similarities between the two types of masks, including such robust features as the high forehead, overhanging eyebrows, multiple lines delineating eyebrows, hairline, and center of the forehead, and the prominent spatula-shaped chin as well as the woven raffia cape embellished with a single cowrie shell. In addition to the many traits the Kete mask shares with the Kuba *bwoom,* its chip-carved surface designs recall a distinctive painted motif characteristic of another Kuba royal mask, *ngaady a mwaash.*   NQ

Provenance: Peter Boyd, Seattle, Washington

POWER AND DISPLAY

FROM THE EARLIEST WRITTEN ACCOUNTS left by Arab and European visitors, we learn of the exploits of African kingdoms and empires in the West African Sudan, the Central African forests, and the East African coastline. Yet since the era of European colonial intervention in the late nineteenth century, not much of this grandeur has survived. While there still remain some highly centralized polities in the sub-Sahara, the vast majority of African people live in simple village-based societies. Regardless of size and complexity, however, African societies generally share a preoccupation with rank and status. This emphasis continues to be the main impetus for technical excellence and innovation in the arts. For objects that indicate or acknowledge prestige, wealth, status, and political power, African peoples resort to a variety of mediums including precious metals. Like people the world over, Africans have a natural inclination to use precious materials conventionally considered to possess intrinsic value, such as gold, silver, and brass or bronze. The Asante gold necklace would, therefore, have conveyed its owner's economic well-being because the metal is treasured in Akan society as a symbol of wealth. Preference for precious metals is predicated on their rarity, aesthetic qualities, and seeming indestructibility, which make them naturally suited for this kind of status investment.

Ownership of prestigious materials is critical to their use. Consequently, the exclusive right exercised by the kings of Benin and Kuba over copper and certain important beads seems inextricably linked to their economic powers. For Benin, research shows that copper, because of its redness, also symbolizes the oba's fiery temperament (Ben-Amos 1980).

The value placed on materials is culturally determined and, as such, may differ from group to group. African cultures appreciate an array of elements—including beads and cowries—to which enormous sentimental and even monetary value is attached. For this reason, these materials are viewed as indexes of social or political distinction. Frequently imported items—for example, trade beads, European brass tacks, buttons, staffs, and medals—easily acquire prestige because of their scarcity. The Yoruba royal footrest or personal "shrine to the head" and the Kuba mask, all profusely embellished with colored beads and cowries, would display their patrons' wealth. There is considerable intermingling of roles in African leadership. The family head, village chief, or sacred king combines in his official functions military, judicial, and priestly duties; he is both a secular and religious figure. Consequently, diverse materials may be employed independently or blended in the manufacture of regalia, each intended to signify a leader's unique attributes and to enhance his effectiveness.

The language of African political symbolism is complex and powerful. Some materials may be preferred for their intrinsic essence, others for their inherent magic powers or nostalgia. Imbued with ancestral significance, some indigenous mediums, such as grasses, natural fibers, raffia, or bark cloth, may be featured in investiture rituals validating political authority. Where an object is composed of more than one material, the multiple statements conveyed about the person may be equally important.

Paramount Chief of Notse town, Togbe Kofi Ahosu, in full ceremonial gear. 1988.

Surface finishing is another important component in objects of display. Superior craftsmanship, as in Western art, is equated with greater value because of the perception that affluent and highly ranked persons can afford the services of the best artists and artisans. Ornamentation and imagery, too, serve a crucial communicative function transmitting complex messages about social status, rank, and authority.

African societies possessing some measure of political sophistication—Benin, Kuba, Asante, and Kongo, for example—are known for the control exerted by their elites on art production. And where royal courts existed, they often attracted the best and most skilled craftspeople, accounting for some of the most exquisite African art pieces. When art objects are employed to proclaim the achievement of status, such as we see in Benin warriors' bronze leopard pendants, in carved wooden staffs of the Kongo elite, or in Luba use of ornate metal ceremonial pipes, the interests of their users are diminished in the face of larger social and political considerations. Utilitarian objects, such as the Central African throwing knife, may also be transformed into symbols, downplaying their original functions and elevating them to display objects. The common thread is that there are often at stake broader ideological issues affecting whole communities when these objects come into play. Consequently, how an emblem is carried and manipulated in the social context, its degree of visibility, and who gets to exploit its symbolic implications is essential to our understanding. This point is exemplified in a variety of illustrated examples: the Akan staff, the Yoruba beaded footrest, the Kuba royal masks (*Ngaady a Mwaash, Mwaash a Mbooy*, and *Mboom*), and the Luba stool. Yet what has to be underscored here, too, is the need to look beyond the superficial decorative medium of a display item and to focus on its underlying components—for instance, the wood, basketry, or raffia frame of a bead crown; the coarse cotton textile that lines the interior of a prestigious velvet or silk garment; or the herbal magical charm, inserted into the king's throne, to list a few. It is in the combinations of these elements that the ruler's power resides.

Awareness of the self is fundamentally important in art creation and use, even though the ordinary African generally receives little attention as a patron of the arts. Yet to be able to appreciate the work of art, consideration of ownership is important, for patronage is intertwined with the precise function, meaning, and significance of the piece (MacGaffey 1990; Raverhill 1994). The finished work of art, in fact, reflects the tastes, preferences, and worldview of the user. And, for many African art patrons, visual forms also help to project self-image and to negotiate roles and relationships with others. Through the vehicle of art quotidian concerns with identity and beautification of the body are met. NQ

44 FEMALE EFFIGY VESSEL

Mangbetu, Zaire
Terracotta
h. 31.1 cm (12 ¹/₄ in.)
The Collection of
Sophie Pearlstein

The Mangbetu of northeastern Zaire were particularly recognized for their fine pottery. This female effigy vessel, used for the drinking of palm wine, is an outstanding example of a classic shape with the addition of a neck in the form of a female head with hair dressed in the distinctive style associated with Mangbetu royalty.

For men and women of the ruling classes, an elongated head was a distinctive mark of beauty. It was so desirable that it was induced in infants by binding the head. In famous drawings done in the early 1870s, King Munza is shown dancing before royal wives whose hair is dressed in a style similar to the one shown on this effigy vessel (Schweinfurth 1874). Herbert Lang, a 1910 visitor to the Mangbetu, commented on the hair style set aside for royal women: "First string was wrapped around the forehead and much of the head. The long hair was then drawn around a basketry frame to produce a halo-like shape. Numerous hairpins of ivory, bone, or metal completed the style" (Schildkrout and Keim 1990, 126).

Bark boxes and musical instruments decorated with human heads were described in the late nineteenth century, and magnificent effigy vessels such as this one were first collected and were made well into the twentieth century (Casti 1891, 1, 194). They are typically made of clay, which fires from a dark grey to a lightish cream color, with the details of body and facial decoration indicated by bold incisions and strokes made on the pottery in its leather-hard state.   MK

Provenance: Marc Felix, Brussels

45 CHIEF'S FOOTREST

Yoruba, Nigeria
Glass beads, fabric
h. 22.9 cm (9 in.)
Faxon Collection

Beads are revered among the Yoruba of Nigeria. Not only are beads imbued with religious significance because of their associations with ancestors and deities but they are also quintessential symbols of Yoruba kingship. Consequently, the embellishment of objects with beads signals a royal connection. This piece may have belonged to a distinctive ensemble that included pillows, garments, flywhisks, staffs, sandals, and a crown. Probably used as a footrest, this work is a fine example of Yoruba bead embroidery that most likely belonged to someone of chiefly status, for a royal connection is clearly conveyed by certain well-known motifs—precious colored beads, a human face with distinctive scars, and the interlace or guilloche pattern—long the prerogative of important Yoruba rulers.

Yoruba kingship history goes back nearly one millennium, based on archaeological evidence from the eleventh-century site of Ife. Divine monarchy is attested to in the rich oral traditions of the Yoruba, and bead use in royal regalia is suggested in early bronze sculptures from Ife and related sites. Modern Yoruba people attach enormous significance to beads in general and to particular ancestral types, such as the acclaimed blue glass beads of ancient Ife. This footrest lacks this significant attribute, for its multicolored embroidery consists wholly of tiny trade beads. According to William Fagg, such "seed beads," as they

are known, began to appear in nineteenth- and twentieth-century Yoruba art (Fagg 1980, 9). This object, therefore, could not have been made before the nineteenth century.

Beads are also imbued with religious significance and could indicate a cult affiliation. With particular bead types bearing special relationships to specific deities. So spiritually valuable is a bead-embroidered object that it is instantly connected to a uniquely endowed person. Yoruba rulers, particularly those claiming descent from their legendary ancestor and originator of their divine kingship, Odudua, are notable bead users, as are specially endowed children, diviners, and cult priests.

The footrest's royal association is further reinforced by the inclusion in its imagery of human faces, each with distinctive vertical scars on either cheek. The scarification and the interlace pattern are both principal motifs of high political status in Yoruba culture. They appear in a variety of leadership contexts, particularly on the royal crown, the single most important item of regalia. When featured in crown imagery, the face motif signifies ancestral sanction

or divine presence, a symbolic validation of the ruler's mystical authority. In addition, the footrest has a prominently embroidered inscription: ADE TI OLORUN DE ENIA KO LE SI or "The crown that god wears no human being can remove" (translation by Rowland Abiodun). This seems like an attempt by the original owner, most likely a Yoruba chief, to appropriate for himself superlative attributes reserved only for god, thereby inflating his spiritual powers. Like other beaded insignia, the footrest iconographically bears the imprint of royalty, ancestral authority, and divine pedigree.

It is difficult, without additional evidence, to ascertain if the footrest contains within it anything other than a simple filling. Considering how Yoruba royal insignia are often invested with potent medicines, it is possible that the footrest may be similarly endowed. This seems logical in view of its embroidered writing, which may well be an admonition to the owner's subjects against the usurpation of his authority.   NQ

Provenance: David Ackley, Ann Arbor, Michigan

⑯ COMB

Akan, Ghana

Wood

25.1 x 8.3 cm

(9 ⁷/₈ x 3 ¹/₄ in.)

The Collection of

Joyce Marie Sims

This type of comb is commonly used by Akan and other Ghanaian women. The purpose of an Akan comb is primarily utilitarian, providing a firm grip on areas of hair that are needed to create a plaited coiffure. The ownership and use of combs cuts across social rank and there are no strictures governing the number of combs a woman may own. Indeed, the quantity possessed by an Akan woman is deemed reflective of her attractiveness, since men often give combs to females as tokens of their affection or appreciation. The only differentiating criterion for the combs may be the materials of which they are made. Combs made of ivory, gold, iron, and even bone have been reported from the area, however they are rare. Those who own such examples would use them solely for important ceremonies. This comb is of the most common variety, made of black-painted wood.

While combs are certainly among the most prosaic of personal art forms, their manufacture is hardly a trivial matter; quality craftsmanship is capable of evoking the same emotions as the symbolism involved. Most Akan combs range in length between four and eighteen inches and in width from one to twelve inches. In view of the broad range in sizes, it is plausible to assume that not all were used in the conventional way, with some employed strictly as ornaments. However, whether made of wood or some precious material, it is the comb's motif, particularly the specific imagery carved on them, that seems to be of critical importance to both the male presenter and the female recipient. While references to clan totems, royal regalia, and the like are common in comb imagery, motifs alluding to male-female relationships seem to dominate on comb handles. Very personal and affectionate subject matter is at the core of the comb's symbolic significance.

Iconographically, this piece belongs to a distinct and broad category incorporating the Akan fertility figure *akuaba*. It would thus be viewed as embodying some widely recognized Akan attributes of physical beauty such as the dark, glossy surface, ringed neck, and thin nose that joins the M-shaped eyebrows. This comb can be further linked to two similar examples in the collection of the National Museum of African Art (Antiri 1974, 33) featuring the peculiar lozenge-shaped head and coiffure combination; the minimal treatment of the upper torso; and the incised checkerboard pattern on the back. By virtue of the striking similarity in style and subject matter, all three combs probably came from the same hand. The grid design that decorates the "dress" of the figure visually recalls a format popular in Akan *adinkra* (funerary cloth) or *Kente* cloth. The hair style, consisting of two plaited hornlike coiffures tied together above the head is commonly used by Akan priestesses.   NQ

Provenance: Donald Morris Gallery, Birmingham, Michigan

THREE ROYAL MASKS One of the greatest ethnic complexes in the sub-Sahara is the Kuba kingdom, estimated to be several centuries old. At its apogee, it occupied a geographical region along the northern limits of the central African savanna, chiefly in the area between the Kasai and the lower Sankuru rivers of the Republic of Zaire. During the last three centuries a massive expansionism embarked upon by successive Kuba kings led to the subjugation of many neighboring populations, now fully assimilated (Vansina 1978, 163-67). Knowledge of pre-twentieth-century Kuba history derives chiefly from the indigenous oral tradition, the exclusive domain of the Bushoong royalty whose members pride themselves on their extraordinary genealogy. The more than 121 Kuba kings puts the monarchy's beginnings at around 500 A.D. However the founding of the present dynasty by Shyaam a Mbul a Ngoong is estimated to be about the first quarter of the seventeenth century (Vansina 1982, 294; Adams 1988, 332-38).

Probably no where else in Africa is mythology so central to kingship ideology as it is among the Kuba. Attempts by the Bushoong royal group to falsify its genealogy have gone hand-in-hand with its use of myths to buttress its absolute right to power. Several Kuba myths of creation exist, but the one most often cited speaks of the Kuba royal ancestor, Woot, who is portrayed as a cultural hero and credited with many significant cultural achievements. This creation myth inspired the three royal masks shown here—*Mboom, Mwaash a Mbooy,* and *Ngaady a Mwaash*. The Mwaash a Mbooy depicts the cultural hero, Woot, while Ngaady a Mwaash is said to depict Mweel, Woot's sister-wife (Cornet 1994). It is Mweel's incestuous relationship with her brother that produced the royal line. But Mweel is also spoken of as a lover of Mboom, thus setting up a contentious relationship between the two men. Royal genealogy is thus tied ultimately to human beginnings, and through the masked performances, royal power is both celebrated and reinforced.

The connection forged between Woot and current Kuba rulers is manifested materially in the Mwaash a Mbooy mask. Even though it shares similarities with Ngaady a Mwaash, the mask has a distinctive imagery and was almost certainly invented to serve the greater purpose of legitimizing royal power. The historical importance of Shamba, progenitor of the Bushoong rulers, parallels the mythical Woot who was also the first man. Like Woot, Shamba is credited with numerous cultural innovations in agriculture and textile weaving. By equating the first monarch with Woot, the Bushoong royal line is appropriating for itself a position of cultural primacy in Kuba culture. Yet sources are unequivocal that Shyaam was a foreigner, the son of a female slave, who, according to historian Jan Vansina, came to power by "stealth and gamble." The Bushoong royals therefore constitute an intrusive element in Kuba society. In view of that background, the parallel being forged between the mythical Woot and the royal progenitor is nothing more than an attempt to validate the lofty position of the Bushoong line in Kuba politics. Despite their outsider status, the Bushoong rulers are historically important in the Kasai-Sankuru river valley, offering, as they have done over the past three centuries, a measure of political stability.

It is doubtful if the history of Kuba masquerading can be reconstructed solely on the basis of formal analysis, however, particular materials employed in the creation of some objects may offer clues to Kuba social and economic history. Cowrie shells and glass beads, for instance, were crucial items in the trade with Europeans, over which the Kuba kings had an absolute monopoly. Such copious application of the two materials would have conveyed the wealth and prestige of Kuba royalty when these masks were used in their original contexts. Yet, there is no explanation of

the particular way in which the Kuba artists used embroidered beads to highlight lips, eyebrows, and the bridge of the nose. Pigments, such as white, black, and ocher replicate color schemes found in Kuba embroidery. Considering its widespread use in Kuba art, this coloration and the painted black-and-white triangular motifs that decorate the Ngaaddy a Mwaash mask may be part of a broad, complex symbolic system. Unlike the other royal masks, the Mboom masks' styling, including the use of copper sheeting, may have been borrowed from Kuba neighbors. Copper sheets were formerly used as currency in the Kasai-Sankuru valley.

Certain elements, however, may be construed as visual metaphors that aid in reinforcing the differences in political status between the mythic Mboom and the privileged Woot and his sister Mweel. Red parrot feathers that accent the protuberance on top of the Mwaash a Mbooy mask are associated with celestial bodies in addition to signifying the ability to communicate with spirits and would thus have alluded to the divinity of the monarch. Similarly, the Mboom mask's fringe of bark or raffia cloth costume sets it apart from the other royal masks which use Kuba designed embroidered cloth. Bark cloth remains a fabric of enormous religious significance and ancestral associations although it is not visible in the regalia of Kuba kings. Yet by wearing the material during investiture rites, young regents symbolically connect the identity of the Mboom to Kuba ancestry (Cornet 1994). Bark cloth also stands in marked contrast to coarse cotton cloth, the latter woven and thus ultimately symbolizing the civilizing influence of Kuba royalty, one of the many claims of the cultural accomplishments of deceased Kuba kings.

Attention also needs to be paid to the specific roles allocated the individual masks in performance, for it is in the context of public ceremonies featuring the three masks that their cultural significance and the interplay of art, myth, and politics are articulated.

The three masks appear on solemn religious occasions, including the funerals of nobles, and also play roles in initiations of Kuba boys into adulthood. Their prominence in puberty rites suggests that boys receive their first dose of royal Kuba ideology during the crucial transition to adulthood. The mask's appearances on diverse occasions demonstrates the extent to which the particular political philosophy of the Bushoong rulers permeates critical areas of Kuba social life.

Artistic innovations, unparalleled in Kuba history, are said to have taken place during the "Age of Kings," roughly the late eighteenth through the nineteenth centuries, when enormous wealth flowed to the Bushoong court from its monopoly over local and long distance trade. The Bushoong rulers, as chief patrons of the arts, exerted a magnetic pull on artists both within and outside the greater Kuba kingdom. As Kuba kings extended their authority well beyond the Kasai-Sankuru region, the period saw the assimilation of diverse neighboring art-producing groups, such as the Kongo and the Kete. The result was a convergence of numerous foreign artistic conventions. The introduction of the royal Mboom masks, which share many striking features of masks produced and used today by the Kete, may yet be one example of the ramifications of this complex historical interaction. The Mboom mask's pronounced, overhanging forehead and exaggerated facial features are considered similar to those of the Twa, believed to be indigenous owners of much of the land now controlled by the Kuba kings. That the Mboom, like the other two royal masks, is decorated with prestige beads closely associated with royal power suggests the modicum of recognition that the non-royal pygmy groups received.

The three masks also incorporate formal elements articulating the history of assimilation and appropriation of cultural influences. Taken together, they show the substantial base of the ruling elite, reflecting its complex

history of economic control. The visual form, with its sophisticated interweaving of media and ornamentation, celebrates a key cultural accomplishment of the Bushoong royalty.

Enormous symbolic value is attached to the opposition between alien rulers and autochthonous populations in many African societies. Many such historical conflicts are known to be reenacted in ritual. The consensus among anthropologists is that these performances serve to periodically revalidate the status quo or to release tensions arising from political rivalries (Fortes 1962; Gluckman in Forde 1962; Goody 1971). The myth of Woot may explain the roles played by the three masked characters in the founding of the kingship. However, taken both individually and as a group, the three royal masks document, albeit in visually cryptic terms, a monarchy's remarkable developmental history. Their triadic relationship is a singular formal and conceptual statement of the subtlety of the ideology of power.   NQ

47. Provenance: Tambaran Gallery, New York
48. Provenance: M. Nemer, Detroit, Michigan
49. Provenance: Tambaran Gallery, New York

⑤⓪ HIP PENDANT

Edo, Benin Kingdom,
Nigeria
Brass, copper
h. 24.1 cm (9 ¹/₂ in.)
Private Collection

In Benin culture, the representation of a leopard is considered the quintessential symbol of royal authority. Its use is a prerogative of royalty and depictions of the animal, from the naturalism of full-figure sculptures to the minimal, abstract modes of teeth necklaces and pelt garments worn by Benin warriors, are pervasive on many kingship items. The leopard face pendant makes reference to the founder of the present line of Benin kings or *obas*, Ewuare (1500-1540), who adopted the leopard as his personal symbol. From a personal emblem, the creature developed into the most pervasive animal motif in Benin kingship iconography by the late nineteenth century.

The earliest known leopard imagery in sub-Saharan Africa comes from the ninth-century site of Igbo Ukwu in eastern Nigeria, indicating the antiquity of certain concepts and practices associated with West African leadership. While the imagery's precise links with kingship remain largely conjectural in the Igbo Ukwu case, there is no doubt that it was probably used by personages in incipient leadership roles. This viewpoint is buttressed by the cultural context in which the objects were discovered, which featured a diverse array of finely cast bronze objects with exceptional ornamentation.

Like most other metal Benin sculptures, this piece was cast by the lost-wax technique. It differs slightly from comparable pendants because of the attachment of bells to the edges of the face. Unlike bronze-cast human face pendants, the leopard images appear to have been restricted to the Edo citizens of the Benin Kingdom, possibly a result of internal politics. The Benin kingdom was highly centralized with its obas exercising tight control over political and economic life. After adopting the leopard as his personal symbol, Ewuare imposed upon his subjects a scarification pattern imitating the creature's characteristic facial marks (Blackmun 1991, 32-33). Benin oral history claims that the purpose of the practice was to aid in identifying Edo subjects, however, it may have been intended to remind Ewuare's subjects of his power and to promote the omnipresence of the monarch.

The leopard is a natural visual metaphor for the king, because of its unique attributes in the display of power. Its appeal stems from its known physical prowess, its notoriety as a ferocious predator, and its cunning disposition. Appropriating these natural traits adds to the mysticism that enshrouds most kingships in sub-Saharan Africa. In the old Benin kingdom, the symbol provided both an umbrella of protection and a veritable vehicle for extending the oba's political control. Evidence from bronze-cast architectural plaques shows that Benin officials wore such pendants on their left hip suspended from belts. Two-dimensional representations on the plaques show incised relief patterns resembling the leopard's pelt on the ceremonial garments and shields of warriors.

The most common depiction of leopards on pendants is a frontal one, and as judged from their appearance on plaques, they were probably intended to be viewed that way to emphasize the animal's marks, eyes, and fangs. The latter are always so clearly defined even on crudely cast pieces that it suggests manipulation of the image as a tool of social control was of central importance. For instance, the omnipresence of the oba and his fiery temperament would have been communicated by the animal's eyes. Benin warriors and other state functionaries decorated with the motif would have been considered as not only acting on behalf of the oba but also, in essence, transporting the spirit of the ruler. Thus while the royal totem gave the wearer power to act in the name of the king, it also may have served to perpetually instill fear in both those who viewed the emblem and those who wore it. After the demise of the Benin kingdom following the British punitive expedition in 1897 and the advent of colonialism, however, leopard pendants ceased to function this way (Blackmun 1991, 28).

The leopard face pendant seems functionally different from those bearing the oba's human face, which were dispersed among Benin's foreign vassals. The ruler of Igala, a kingdom located around the confluence of the Niger and Benue rivers, and the Ibo divine rulers at Oreri and Oguta, also east of the Niger, have examples that have been confirmed as Benin works. It is not known what reasons may have dictated the distribution of different types of pendants other than perhaps an attempt to stress the overlordship of Benin on other polities. The leopard as a political symbol had widespread significance throughout southern Nigeria, and Benin monarchs may have realized that distribution of pendants depicting the animal could enhance rather than curtail the powers of subjugated kings.   NQ

Provenance: Helen and Mace Neufeld; Merton Simpson, New York

51 FEAST SPOON (WUNKIRMIAN)

Dan, Liberia

Wood

h. 41.9 cm (16¹/₂ in.)

Private Collection

Among the Dan, a Mande-speaking group in northeastern Liberia, the large wooden spoon used to serve rice during communal feasts is called a *wunkirmian* and is used by the *wunkirle,* the chosen leader of the women of the village. At a feast, the wunkirle leads an entourage of women around to offer everyone some rice, using the spoon to dig the food out of a large bowl. The bowl of such a spoon is said to represent a belly that is "pregnant with rice" (Fischer and Himmelheber 1984, 123), perhaps symbolizing the fertility of both the land and its inhabitants.

Leadership among the village women is only one quality of a wunkirle; more important are her generosity and hospitality. Honorable guests, groups of traveling entertainers, and other visitors are directed to go to her house for food and accommodation for however long they wish. The spoon is not only an emblem of the wunkirle's generosity, but also recognition of her productivity. She must be resourceful to maintain a constant supply of food and a large well-kept house. As the village leader, she assumes responsibility for preparing meals at communal farming activities.

These customs are deeply rooted in Dan farming tradition, and the spoons are passed down from generation to generation. Continuation of such a communally significant custom is secured by the wunkirle choosing her successor during her lifetime. The successor is said to be notified in a dream both of her status and of the location of the spoon (Fischer and Himmelheber 1984, 124). At the death of an old wunkirle, a memorial festival is held, and at this time the new wunkirle must prove her generosity and reinforce the power of her wunkirmian by preparing a large feast and giving gifts.

The handles of some spoons depict a female head, a stylized representation of the original owner showing essential individual features, such as scarification and coiffure, rather than a portrait likeness. As a spoon is passed down over several generations, the portrait is regarded as an ancestor whose spiritual presence oversees and protects the villagers. Spoons with legs, such as this example, are called *megalumia* and "are said to represent legs of all the people arriving on foot to be fed by the *wunkirle*" (Johnson 1986, 20). This piece also shows the Dan ideal of women's beauty with powerful legs, muscular buttocks, and slender torsos.

Similar to the Dan masks, the spoons are manifestations of a spirit that helps an individual in her tasks. Once there has been a ritualized dedication and a sacrifice offered to inaugurate a newly carved spoon, it becomes a sacred object and is believed to possess a will to move on its own. When not in use, the spoon is kept hanging on the wall in the wunkirle's house and no one else may touch it. Anyone who violates this rule—even by mistake—must provide a large animal for the next feast.   CTM

Provenance: Thomas B. Stauffer and Charles Fox, San Francisco, California

㊾ EFFIGY VESSEL

artist: Voania of Muba
(d. 1928), Kongo
Terracotta
43.2 x 26 cm (17 x 10 ¼ in.)
The Detroit Institute of Arts
Founders Society Purchase
with funds from the Friends
of African and African
American Art, the Arthur
D. Coar Endowment Fund,
Joseph H. Boyer Memorial
Fund, and the Henry E.
and Consuelo S. Wenger
Foundation Fund
(1994.47)

The Kongo ceramicist Voania of Muba was a master at symbolism, expertly integrating figures into simple pottery forms. The widely shared belief that the head serves as a conduit through which spirits enter and exit the human body may have partly inspired this effigy vessel. By placing the vessel's spout in the area of the crown of the equestrian figure, Voania turns the torso into a conduit through which ritual drink could have been channeled to the receptacle beneath, echoing the importance of the head in Kongo religious thought.

In his work, Voania interweaves the indigenous and the foreign. His human figures frequently wear European attire, usually the typical late-nineteenth-century coat with a short collar and varieties of imported caps. Buttons, often clearly depicted, leave no ambiguity in the mind of the viewer about the artist's intention to stress these emblems. These distinctive foreign attributes are recognized attributes of the Kongo elite, probably introduced by Europeans during their historical contact with the Kongo.

Prestige, wealth, and status are key issues raised by this equestrian image. The rider's enormous head, together with his enlarged upper body, give additional emphasis to his Western clothing. The mounted figure makes a statement about the economic and political status of the person being memorialized on the vessel. It is difficult to place this vessel within the larger scheme of Kongo art, especially in terms of function. It is not unlike other works since figural pottery is well known, however, Voania's style and approach to figural depiction and his iconographic approach evidently depart from established Kongo norms. Iconographically, he limits his field to only a handful of motifs to include equestrian images, standing couples, and single human busts.

Although well celebrated in the West, Voania was hardly known within the Cabinda region in western Zaire where he practiced his art. According to the most detailed biography of the artist written by Zdenka Volavka (1977, 65), Voania's different approach made his works less appealing to his own people, who were quick to dismiss it as not of their own. Voania benefitted in many ways from his

contact with Europeans to whom he looked for patronage. His fine pots were never used locally by his African kinsfolk but were shipped to Europe as early as 1888, a practice that probably continued until his death in 1928. Voania used technical methods that did not radically depart from the traditions of Bakongo hand-made ceramics. Both the main body and figurative superstructure were sculpted by hand.

Ritual pottery is considered as more or less sculpture, although Voania may have carried this concept to extremes, for unlike its traditional Kongo equivalents, this piece sacrifices utility for symbolism. In addition to his exploitation of imagery over functionality, Voania's characteristic signing of his pieces places them among a unique corpus of African art works. On this piece, the artist used incised lines to form multiple enclosed spaces on the shoulder of the vessel into which he inscribed his name, "Voania," and his town, "Muba." Although it is not clear if this decorative signature was used in earlier works, it is well known that Voania began autographing his vessels around the turn of the century (Leuzinger 1978, 190). The story goes that the illiterate Voania was taught how to write his name,

probably by Dr. Elie J. Etienne, the one-time director of the Musée Royal de l'Afrique Centrale. Voania himself never sold his works directly to outsiders nor did he visit any of the pottery markets to promote his art.

It would appear that Voania, the "prolific" artist that he is known as today, is a creation of the West. This external validation may have had a domino's effect, encouraging a phenomenal increase in the artist's output. Evidence suggests that the expansion of his patronage probably prompted some faking of his works as others artists attempted to master his technique and signature. The question remains whether it was the artist's intention to start a new art genre. Yet, even if he worked solely for the tourist market, there is no question that he showed in his finished works a unique sensitivity to Kongo sensibilities regarding representation.   NQ

Provenance: Collection of Robert F. Thompson; Alan Brandt, New York.

cannabis (which is refined to produce hemp) originated in Asia, an Arab connection is plausible, although the substance could have been introduced to East Africa by Indians or other Middle Eastern peoples. The entry of cannabis into Africa is dated to the middle of the thirteenth century, while tobacco was most likely introduced in the sixteenth century by European traders who obtained the plant from the Americas (Philips 1983, 315-17).

Pipes such as this one are thought to have been used for hemp smoking, because ethnographic reports maintain that cannabis and hemp have always been smoked, while tobacco is more likely to have been snuffed or chewed (Philips 1983, 316).

The precise functions of figural pipes, however, are difficult to determine. They may have been used for healing purposes since sculptures of females holding bowls (instead of sitting atop pipe bowls) are connected with divination practices (Nooter 1991, 23). Nonetheless, the image of the female as pipe stem recalls the convention of the female as stool support. In each case, the female figure is necessary for the function of the kingly attribute, as women have always been necessary for the growth and mainte-nance of the Luba kingdom.   LBH

Provenance: Marc Felix, Brussels

53 CEREMONIAL PIPE

Luba, Zaire
Wood, metal
h. 54.8 cm (21 ²/₃ in.)
Anonymous Loan

The female figure is widespread in Luba art, perhaps because of the prominent role of women in the Luba creation myth, as well as their acknowledged role in Luba political history. The relationship of women to Luba kings is most commonly depicted artistically in the form of stools, with the seat usually supported by a carved figure of a kneeling woman. This has been interpreted as a sign of servitude (Flam 1971, 56-57), but it could also be read as the recognition of the privileged role of women in the formation and perpetuation of the kingdom. In fact, women are figured on many items of royal regalia, including headrests, staffs, ceremo-nial axes, and pipes. The female figures carved on pipes are stylistically similar to the stool figures.

Figural pipes most often consist of a bowl with a stem in the form of a kneeling female. The stem continues through and above the figure's head. The hair is usually carefully styled and the body is carved with scarification patterns. These characteristics refer to a woman of high social standing, such as one in the service of the court. They also mark the pipe as an appropriate attribute of the king. The lozenge-shaped patterning on the figure may also refer to the idea of secret knowledge, of which women are regarded as primary guardians. On this pipe, the gesture of the woman holding her hands up to her breasts indicates possession and care of royal secrets of the king and his female advisors (Nooter 1993, 100 and 105).

While figural pipes may have been used for tobacco smoking, it is also possible that they were used for hemp; similarly shaped pipes have shown up in excavations across Africa with evidence of that usage (Philips 1983, 309). Hemp most likely was introduced in Africa by Arab smokers arriving on the coast of the Indian Ocean. Because

54 CARYATID STOOL

Hemba, Zaire
Wood, rope
47 x 22.9 cm
(18 ¹/₂ x 9 in.)
Private Collection

The widespread dispersion of caryatid stools among the ethnic groups of northeastern Zaire is generally attributed to the earlier expansion of Luba influence. While the use, iconography, and style of such stools have been well researched for the Luba, less is known for neighboring groups. Hemba lands adjoin those of the Luba, and in the period of greatest Luba political expansion, some of the Hemba chiefdoms were absorbed into the Luba kingdoms, while others emulated aspects of their rule. This accounts for much of the stylistic similarity in the sculptural production of both groups.

However, traditional Hemba society is less stratified, and the political system less centralized than that of the Luba. Furthermore, while the Luba recognize certain features of their matrilineal kin groups, they are patrilineally organized, but the Hemba practice dual descent. These considerations are particularly important in assessing the role of the female figure in Hemba art, as they may suggest alternative interpretations for the importance of prestige objects generally and representations of female figures specifically.

Luba stools with female figures have complex political associations (Nooter 1987 and 1991, passim). Once thought to be strictly a chiefly prerogative, caryatid stools were also associated with the semi-secret *Mbudye* society that functioned as a counterbalance to the ruler's authority (Nooter in Phillips 1995, 292). Therefore, the elevated position of the person seated upon the stool was evocative of two distinct categories of power. Unfortunately, it is not clear whether caryatid stools were also emblematic of different branches of authority in Hemba contexts. For both the Luba and the Hemba, the stool was an important symbol of legitimacy, although it was rarely used in public. Luba informants sometimes interpret the female figure as a depiction of a past ruler, reflecting the belief that rulers were reincarnated as women, but again, it is not clear that the Hemba shared this belief (Nooter 1984, 4-5). Clearly the swollen abdomen is suggestive of the perpetuation of the ruling lineage.

Given the importance of the matrilineage in Hemba society, the caryatid may have been intended as a depiction of a particular female ancestor. Because ancestors are thought to play a crucial role in the lives of their decendants, offering benevolent protection in return for proper respectful offerings, the figure's actual role as supporting the ruler may reflect the ancestor's burden of insuring the well-being of the living (Flam 1971, 59). The Hemba are renowned for their large sculptures depicting male ancestors, most of which display the same prized attributes of composure and dignity present in the stool's caryatid. The male ancestor figures were frequently clad in a cloth or vegetal wrapper, and the cord around the waist of this female figure probably once attached a covering. It seems likely that these wrappers served as another reflection of the modesty and decorum that still characterize Hemba social behaviors.

The scarification, bracelets, and carefully delineated cruciform headdress in this example are all suggestive of a person of rank. For the Luba, elaborate scarification was an essential attribute of female beauty and sexual attraction; without it a woman was considered ineligible for both marriage and spirit possession (Nooter 1991, 240).

Whether these associations were also held by the Hemba is uncertain, but it is clear that scarification was an important aspect of feminine beauty. At puberty, young women underwent a period of seclusion during which they learned the techniques of scarification and the deliberate elongation of the genitals, which is also apparent in this figure.

Finally, the distinctive hair style worn by the figure is well documented in the historical accounts of the Hemba and is frequently depicted on both male and female figures. Its exact significance is unknown, however, although its cruciform pattern may have cosmological links with the passage of the sun and moon (Neyt in Herreman and Petridis 1993, 180). Carefully plaited and arranged over a cane frame, the hair style was time-consuming to complete and was probably originally a sign of rank and prestige.

PM

Provenance: Donald Morris Gallery, Birmingham, Michigan

55 MUDPACK HEADDRESS (EMEDOT)

Karamojong,
Uganda, Kenya
Earth, pigment,
ostrich feathers,
human hair, beads
26 x 25.4 cm
(10 1/4 x 10 in.)
The Collection of Dede
and Oscar Feldman

The Karamojong are a semi-nomadic people, structuring their lives around the raising and herding of cattle. They also grow some grains, but since the group is not sedentary and much of the area is semi-arid, planting and harvesting crops is a secondary activity.

Authority among the Karamajong is divided according to generations and then into smaller age groups with the eldest set holding the most power. The elders are responsible for leading most ritual performances and have decision-making powers affecting the entire group. The next generation group is that of warrior. In the past it was common for the Karamajong to have to defend their herds and also raid for cattle depending on the needs of the group. There were also frequent conflicts with neighboring groups over pasture land. Thus, the warrior generation is an important one, for the welfare of the entire group sometimes depends upon them. At all times there are two generational groups, and the passage of power from one generation to the next takes place approximately every thirty-five years. It is usually pressure from the younger set to obtain more power from the older one that brings on the transfer. Coiffures play an important role in this

context, serving to identify groups and helping to reinforce solidarity among set members.

Although descriptions of Karamojong hairstyling techniques are lacking, observations of the closely related Suk reveal a complex process of hairstyling that includes twisting short plaits across the skull. As the hair grows, it is mixed with clay and shaped into a pad on top of the head. While the clay is still wet, sockets of gut or cow teats are inserted into it to hold ostrich feathers. The colors of the feathers, as well as of the painted lines along the edge of the chignon, indicate the stages of training through which a warrior must pass (Adamson 1967, 21-22).

Elders wear a flat, tonguelike headdress placed on the back of the head and extending down the back by as much as four feet. A pre-initiation headdress worn by young men consists of an elongated cone bound with closely coiled string at the back of the head. Headdresses can function as a sign of individuality in the particulars of design and patterning. This type of headdress is probably that of an older age-set individual.

Coiffures also reinforce concepts of initiated males' role in society, for "intricately coifed hair is a sign of masculinity, courage, and strength" (Arnoldi and Kraemer 1995). The use of ostrich feathers suggests strength. Ostriches are found in the area, have no natural enemies, and are quite dangerous, attacking if threatened. Elaborate coiffures with a large array of feathers can also take

on the characteristics of a lion's mane.

Men take great pride in their coiffures, which are often prepared for special ceremonial occasions. These intricate hair styles result in men carrying headrests with them almost everywhere they go so as not to damage the coiffure. The headrests are also fashioned according to age groups and are made by their eventual users. Until 1971, it was common for Karamajong males to wear coiffures and possibly some other items such as wrist and finger knives and a leopard cape. However, the government of Uganda established laws making it illegal to wear bangles, coiffures, and other traditional attire and required people to wear clothing of manufactured cloth.

The origins of the coiffure may be traced to similar forms in ancient Egypt. The original Karamojong group is believed to have migrated from the northeast in present-day Ethiopia, making such a connection possible. Karamojong artifacts have been noted to bear a highly stylized and disciplined pattern. Notable among these are headdresses and the stool/headrests which bear an uncanny resemblance to some of the headdresses and headrests of ancient Egypt (Wilson 1973, 81-93).   RV

 **CAMEL SADDLE**
(TAMSAK)

Tuareg, Mali or Niger

Leather covered wood,

silver, copper, brass

78.7 x 39.4 x 63.5 cm

(31 x 15 1/2 x 25 in.)

The Detroit Institute of Arts

Founders Society

Purchase with funds

from the Friends of

African and African

American Art, the

African, Oceanic and

New World Cultures

General Fund, Mr. and

Mrs. Allan Shelden

III Fund, Henry E. and

Conseulo W. Wenger

Foundation fund,

and funds from Russell

J. Cameron, and Dr.

and Mrs. Bryce Alpern

(1994.23)

The Tuareg are nomadic livestock breeders living throughout the western Sahara and northwestern Sudan regions, primarily in Mali, Algeria, Niger, and Burkina Faso. These regions are surrounded by the Aār and Hoggar Mountains which afford these nomadic people protection from the outside world. The Tuareg are also known as the "people of the veil" or "the blue people" names derived from the traditional Tuareg style of dress that includes a veil and headdress made of cotton cloth. The cloth is often dyed with indigo, which stains the skin and leaves it bluish. The Tuareg have clung tightly to their traditional dress as well as many other customs (Slavin 1973, 38). Tuareg nomads still depend largely on camels for transportation. A mark of prestige, the camel is of vital importance in the affairs and trade of the Tuareg.

When camels reach the age of three, they are trained as either pack or saddle animals. This saddle is a *tamsak*, an object of great prestige used not on the caravan trail but for camel races, festivals, or short journeys. The pommel on these saddles extends forward, ending in a type of cross. The Tuareg also use a simpler saddle called a *tahyast,* or *tahiacht,* that does not have a cross pommel and is used primarily for work or for training.

The cross pommel not only distinguishes the tamsak, but is also functional, allowing the rider a measure of stability. It has been suggested that the pommel of the tamsak recalls the shape of the cross of Agadez,

which is commonly found among the Tuareg. "The masculine sex, the pommel of the camel saddle, and the four cardinal directions are represented by the cross," according to Nancy Mickelson (1976, 18). Agadez is a town originally established as one of the most important markets on ancient caravan trading routes, linking north Africa with that south of the Sahara.

Elaborate silver and leather surface decorations also distinguish the *tamsak* and make them objects reflecting prestige, wealth, and high social status. A saddle may be highly stylized or relatively simple in appearance depending on both the artist and the patron. In studies of the leather working traditions of the western Sudan, it has been noted that most craftspeople of the region "do not mass-produce goods for sale but rather work on items commissioned directly by clients . . . the creation of the object can draw on the experience of both artist and patron" (Frank 1987, 54).

All leather work and metalsmithing are done by women and men, respectively, who are members of a caste of the Tuareg called the *inaden.* According to anthropologist Susan Rasmussen, Tuareg smiths "have access to indirect power through their control of unofficial negotiations surrounding marriage and politics, through their secret language called *Tenet,* and in their allegedly special relationship to the fire *djinn,*" or evil spirits (Rasmussen 1992, 105).   ON

Provenance: Reynold Kerr, New York

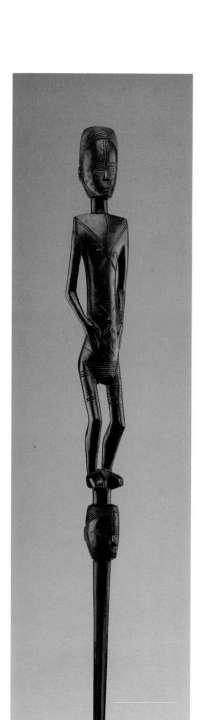

57 STAFF FIGURE

Malungu or Rungu

Zaire and Zambia

Wood

h. 48.3 cm (19 in.)

Private Collection

The Malungu plateau or massif in eastern Zaire is located within a region inhabited by various fairly autonomous peoples broadly known as Tabwa. The inhabitants of the massif area share linguistic and historical ties with both the core Tabwa peoples to the north and the Bemba to the south. The Marungu massif has seen periodic influxes of culturally distinct peoples for centuries. Sometimes following game, sometimes fleeing slave traders, and sometimes expanding their political spheres, these groups have included the Nyamwezi, Zimba, and Bemba. Ethnic identifications in this region are imprecise and vary dynamically with the social and historical circumstances of a given individual, lineage, or village (Maurer and Roberts 1985, 5-9). Not surprisingly, the arts of this region are stylistically varied, often showing affinities with works created by geographically distant peoples. The ethnic designation for this staff connotes less a distinct set of cultural ideas and preferences (although these may exist), than a probable geographic origin for its manufacture.

Staffs were owned by both chiefs and diviners among the Tabwa, serving as emblems of their status and powers. When a chief entered a building, he would often plant his staff in the ground outside to signify both his presence and his continuing vigilant protection of his people. Certain divination rituals also included the planting of a staff into the ground. Bundles of medicinal substances and bells attached to the top would indicate the presence of invisible sorcerers. Frequently, Janus-oriented heads were rendered on staffs to suggest the owner's encompassing vision (Maurer and Roberts 1985, 169).

In this example, both heads face forward, which may be suggestive of the pervasive duality associated with Tabwa chiefs. The chief embodies the ability to impart wisdom to his people, enabling them to perceive and prepare for danger, and the most potent of sorcerers' powers, therefore symbolically personifing the balance between good and evil, light and darkness (Maurer and Roberts 1985, 26). This same idea of balance is visually expressed in the vertical scarification line that divides the body in Tabwa art, seen here on the figure's chest (Maurer and Roberts 1985, 28).

Through the meeting of carefully incised lines down the forehead and above the eyes both heads on this staff emphasize the point immediately above the nose. This is the locus of wisdom in Tabwa thinking, the point of origin for the special vision associated with dreams and divination. This point is symbolically linked with the navel through the continuation of the body's midline to suggest the intellect and fertility that are combined within the individual (Maurer and Roberts 1985, 35).

Tabwa staffs, like those of the Luba people to the west, usually feature female figures. Since descent is traced through the chief's sister, women are important for the continuation of the chiefly line. However, in another dualistic opposition, they may be regarded by men as potentially dangerous or deceitful (Maurer and Roberts 1985, 34). Their presence on staffs surely connotes links with female ancestors but also suggests their necessary role as the male counterpart, completing the life cycle.

Despite the many iconographic references which this staff shares with most Tabwa sculpture, it should be noted that it is stylistically distinct from the great majority of known Tabwa works. In the catalogue prepared for the exhibition "Tabwa: The Rising of a New Moon," only one other work closely resembles this piece (Maurer and Roberts 1985, fig. 402). Now in the Stanley Collection in Iowa, it is also a female-figured staff. The two share not only specific details of scarification and hair style, but also the elongation of the cylindrical heads and the pose with slightly bent legs. The resemblance between these works is similar enough to suggest a distinctive regional substyle, indicative perhaps of a single artist or workshop.   PM/DR

Provenance: Marc Felix, Brussels

58 PAIR OF ANTHROPOMORPHIC HARPS

Ngbaka, Zaire
Wood, hide, beads
h. 64.8 cm; 63.5 cm
(25 ¹/₂ in.; 25 in.)
The Collection of Sidney
and Madeline Forbes

The Ngbaka peoples reside in the northernmost section of Zaire, although the group is thought to have originally migrated from the northwest near Lake Chad (Koloss 1990, 78). The whole of northern Zaire has experienced a great deal of cultural interplay as a result of migrations of different groups into the area. Harps were brought into this region from northeastern Africa, and several of the instruments are based on Egyptian forms (Waschmann 1964). In this part of Africa, harps are exclusively played by men, who often accompany themselves with song and stories. Many harpists travel from village to village, even to ones outside their ethnic group, causing similar features to appear on instruments from different locations. Harps may have been made in one area and used in another.

Some unique features distinguish Ngbaka harps from those of other groups. The entire figure is used on the Ngbaka instruments, sometimes with such added touches as pubic hair to lend the creation a physical connection to humans. The large, heavy-set legs are another distinctive feature. Harps similar in form to these two but probably from a neighboring group have legs that are much more slender and segmented. The solidity of the legs allowed the harp to be beaten on the ground; rattling beads produced additional sounds. Yet another feature of the Ngbaka harps is the treatment of the head. Although slight variations exist and other forms are sometimes employed, the face is usually carved simplistically and topped with a helmet-type coiffure. Other types show a coiffure with plaits of hair running from the front of the head to the back. This is hinted at by the lines painted on the head of the Detroit male figure.

These harps represent a male and female pair called *apostrophy seti* by the Ngbaka in reference to the groups belief in the primordial couple Seto and Nabo. It is believed that when the harps are played, the couple become the harps and sing music for the audience. Legends of Seto refer to him as a happy, carefree character who enjoys women and often plays tricks on others but not in a mean-spirited way. It is also said that he taught men how to sing and dance. Nabo is mentioned as both his sister and his wife. Together, the pair are associated with fertility, prosperity, and bringing good harvests and hunting (Seattle Art Museum 1984). Seto is also the central figure in many cults, particularly those of initiation (Neyt 1981, 24). The white pigment on these harps probably makes reference to ancestral spirits and acknowledges Seto and Nabo as the original ancestors.   RV

Provenance: Marc Felix, Brussels

59 CEREMONIAL THROWING KNIFE

Konda, northeastern Zaire

Iron, wood

h. 59.1 cm (23 1/4 in.)

Private Collection

Throughout the continent of Africa, knives have a wide variety of uses as arms, symbols of power, currency, and ceremonial emblems. Although the specific function of this knife, known as a throwing knife, is not clear, when closely examined the blades reveal few signs of use or sharpening, which might indicate a ceremonial function. Furthermore, the shape of this knife shows a high level of stylization and a unique sense of balance and symmetry.

While balance and symmetry are necessary components for an object to function as a projectile, high stylization is not. In reference to a parade sword also attributed to the Konda, it has been noted that: "to the Konda of Central Zaire . . . would go the prize for the most ornate and extravagant sword-blade design of all: it is awesome and ostentatious, but totally unsuited for warfare" (Meyer 1995, 127). In this region of central Africa, weapons did not always function as instruments of attack or defense, but rather were often indications of social rank. Similarly, throwing knives were likely to have been designed as marks of office or prestige. They have been known to be used as bride price and "as integral parts of the costumes worn at initiation ceremonies and other rituals" (Spring 1993, 70).

It is also possible that forms and styles of weaponry were shared and borrowed between various groups. The Ngombe and Monzombo in the region of the Zaire River basin have been noted to have sickle-shaped swords. This "diversity of shape, materials and decoration in weaponry from adjacent geographical areas . . . may derive from the need to declare ethnic identity by visual means" (Spring 1993, 85-86).   ON

Provenance: Merton Simpson, New York

⑥⓪ NECKREST

Twa, Zaire
Wood
15.2 x 25.4 cm
(6 x 10 in.)
Private Collection

Of pygmy stock, the Twa are one of the ethnic groups absorbed into the greater Kuba complex in Zaire. Virtually nothing is known of the early religion or material culture of the Twa, who were nomadic hunters. There are very few published Twa sculptural pieces, which suggests either that carving is not widespread or that Twa pieces are mistakenly attributed to neighboring groups. Most examples, like this one, are neckrests supported by Janus-oriented caryatid figures. The striking similarities between this piece and those in two other collections (Eiteljorg and Joss) suggest that they are the products of the same artist. In all three, the caryatids are depicted as half figures, and the connecting piece is richly ornamented with incised geometric patterns. The heads are large with regard to the bodies, and the oversized round eyes are further emphasized by the scarification patterns that lead from their outer edges to the ears. Although facial scarification was practiced by several pygmy groups, its significance for the Twa is unknown.

The use of neckrests was widespread in sub-Saharan Africa, and finely carved examples were usually reserved for persons of higher socioeconomic status. By holding the head off the sleeping mat, neckrests helped to preserve the elaborate hair styles often symbolic of rank. As importantly, they were an effective means for keeping cool, since they allowed air to circulate around the face through the night.

Although several pygmy groups have been described as maintaining distinctive hair styles, it is not clear that these would require such an object for maintenance. Given the egalitarian structure of traditional Twa society, it is also difficult to determine the patrons for such elaborate objects. Since families were forced to move frequently in search of game, household furnishings were traditionally kept to a minimum. This suggests that the production of these figural neckrests originated some time after the establishment of the Kuba kingdom, when the Twa began to settle permanently in villages.

The extent of Kuba cultural influence on the Twa is difficult to ascertain. The relations between the groups are complex, alternating throughout history between animosity and semi-dependence. Several versions of the Kuba's genesis myths and histories recount hostile encounters during the period of the Kuba migrations, and both the Kuba and the Twa recognize the latter as the original inhabitants of the region. This indigenous status makes the Twa important in the installation rites of Kuba chiefs and kings and accords them certain privileges, particularly with regard to hunting and fishing (Vansina 1978, 55). The Twa are renowned hunters, and in addition to trading meat for agricultural products, they have long maintained a representative at the Kuba royal court who is charged with presenting tribute from the hunt (Cornet 1975, 94). But despite centuries of contact, the Twa have apparently not adopted the strongly centralized political systems of their neighbors (Vansina 1978, 4-6).

The somewhat ambiguous character of their relations with the Kuba groups may explain the distinctive features present in the Twa neckrest. The finely carved Twa caryatids are replaced in most Kuba examples with non-figural supports. Conceived as opposing angles, these supports nevertheless create a similar visual effect to the forward thrust of the figures in the Twa piece (Dewey 1993). Finally, the intricate geometric patterning on the supporting bar is reminiscent of the ornamentation found on much Kuba carving, although whether the Twa examples can be interpreted as stylized references to animals, embroidery, or scarification is unclear.   PM

Provenance: Overmeere-Donck, Belgium; Marc Felix, Brussels

61 FLY WHISK

Kwere, Tanzania
Wood, hair
l. 77.5 cm.;
handle 15.9 cm
(30¹/₂ in; 6¹/₄ in.)
The Collection of
Charles, Gail, and
Lyndsay McGee

The small abstract human figure that adorns the handle of this fly whisk is called *Mwana hiti*, whose presence signifies the sacredness of the object. In northeast Tanzania, particularly among the Kwere and Zaramo peoples along the coast, Mwana hiti were found with all kinds of objects, including utilitarian implements. They disappeared from use in the early part of this century in the wake of European colonization and subsequent independence movements.

There is considerable variety in the interpretation and use of the figure, which could represent a fetus, a baby, a young girl, a woman, a man, a husband, an old lady, the primordial ancestor, the clan founder, or the spirit of the clan founder—depending upon the needs of the users. For instance, for a woman who was having difficulty in conceiving, it would represent a hoped-for baby, and the woman would carry the figure on her back under her dress.

Mwana hiti also had a close association with the initiation of girls into womanhood. The wooden figurine was used as a child or a husband to instruct a young girl how to take care of her future family while in seclusion for initiation rites. During the ritual dancing of the initiation ceremony, the title holders of the community displayed their status symbols, such as staffs and whisks, many of which were adorned with Mwana hiti. At the coming-out ceremonies for the initiate, one of her aunts would lead the dance, wielding a fly whisk topped by Mwana hiti. When the initiate returned home from the ceremony and seclusion, she was seated outside, greeting all well-wishers from a ritual clan stool that might have been crowned with Mwana hiti.

Among the Kwere and Zaramo peoples, matrilineal lineage determined the inheritance of farming land. Therefore, the birth of girls and their development into adulthood were particularly celebrated. One translation of the term Mwana hiti is "the daughter of the chair," which may refer to the ritual stool used at the end of the initiation period, or to the throne belonging either to a chief, usually a man, or to some other important person and symbolizing their authority status. The high back on a typical throne depicts a stylized representation of a woman with crested coiffure and small breasts, which are some of the characteristics typical of Mwana hiti. Thus the figure on the throne embodied an ancestral mother whose spiritual power reinforced the authority of the chief to whom the chair belonged.

Similarly, the fly whisk was a status emblem for male and female title holders in a community, as well as being a ritual object and diviner's implement for medicine. The Detroit example is rare for its intricate geometrical design on the handle. It has been suggested that similar geometrical designs rendered on the high back of clan stools is related to popular bodily decoration among the neighboring Hehe women (Roy 1987). Differences in designs for body adornment, such as painting and scarification, may have functioned as identification of a lineage or village. Due to the presence of fine designs suggesting lineage identification and Mwana hiti signifying sacredness, this fly whisk is likely to have belonged to a lineage head or other title holder.

Lineage heads in a matrilineal tribe in Zaire possessed fly whisks of buffalo tails with carved wooden handles. Fly whisks made of sheep or goat hair were wielded during the circumcision ritual in another area in Zaire. Since Zaire is an inland neighbor of Tanzania along the trade route and people in both countries use the Bantu language, they might have had similar customs concerning fly whisks. The kind of hair used in this example is unknown, but the animal may have had significance associated with power and leadership.   CTM

Provenance: Charles Fox, San Francisco, California

62 PAIR OF WHISTLES

Chokwe, Angola
Wood
(L.) h. 10.2 cm (4 in.);
(R.) h. 9.5 cm (3 ³/₄ in.)
The Collection of Dede and Oscar Feldman

The Chokwe people of Angola number about 600,000 and are grouped in loosely organized chiefdoms. Chokwe men are primarily occupied with forest hunting, while women are almost totally involved with farming and related activities. The symbolic importance of hunting is suggested by the many carvings of Tshibinda Ilunga, a famous ruler and hunter of the eighteenth century. His images are central to Chokwe art, and he is traditionally shown with a rifle in one hand and a staff in the other.

Of the many utilitarian objects owned by great hunters, none are more beautifully carved and fashioned than whistles which frequently display elaborate coiffures. Although simple in structure, they are capable of a great range of sound inflections by the stopping and half-stopping of the two holes that protrude like arms just above the whistle opening, and are played with two fingers.

These beautifully carved objects not only enhance the prestige of the hunter but also are frequently attached to spears and other weapons serving as charms to attract game and improve the owner's skills (Bastin 1982, figs. 131, 132).   MK

Provenance: Donald Morris Gallery, Birmingham, Michigan

63 LIDDED BOX

Kuba, Zaire

Wood

h. 22.9 cm (9 in.)

The Collection of

Samuel Thomas, Jr.

In addition to the exquisite masks representing the mythical founders of their kingdom, the Kuba peoples are renowned for their carving. With the exception of small portraits of kings, most carving is devoted to the production of objects for daily use. Like the masks, these cups, beakers, and lidded boxes commonly feature lavish geometric patterning and often assume anthropomorphic or zoomorphic forms. More unusual are boxes such as this one, modeled after traditional lidded baskets.

Generally carved from a single block of wood, boxes were used to store jewelry, razors, and most commonly *tukula*, a reddish substance made from the powdered bark of an indigenous tree. Known as *tool* (or *twool*) amongst the Bushoong, tukula served a variety of purposes and was perceived as having some magical efficacy (Cornet 1971, 143). Used as a dye for hair or cloth, it was also employed as a cosmetic in certain ritual contexts. Tukula figured in burial rites, where it was rubbed on the body of the deceased (Kecskési 1987, 332). In addition, it was often mixed with sand and oil to

form a thick paste known as *bongotol,* which women modeled into small figurines for placement in burials or as mementos of the deceased (Cornet 1971, 143-44).

These various uses of tukula afford one explanation for the elaborate carved boxes. Another lies in the nature of the Kuba's social and political structure. Organized into a highly stratified bureaucracy centered around the Bushoong king, Kuba society is dominated by nobles and titled men who vigorously compete for power and prestige. Visual displays of wealth are thus extremely important proclamations of status and stimulate lively artistic production. Professional woodcarvers are well-patronized, and innovation and ornamentation are particularly valued (Vansina 1982, 74).

The repair evident on this example attests to its value as a prized possession; like many fine old pieces, once broken it was not discarded, but carefully rejoined and fastened with twine and metal. It is rather large in comparison with many other tukula boxes, and its intricate low-relief patterning suggests that it required many hours to complete. The surface motifs, drawn mostly from the splendid raffia weavings and embroideries for which the Kuba are also famous, all have individual

names. While the body of the box is symmetrically arranged in two broad registers of diamond-shaped designs, the sides of the lid display a shifting of patterns within identical triangular frames. The decorative program attests to the Kuba's extraordinary mastery of geometric variation (Adams 1978, 24-25).

Perhaps the most interesting feature of the work is the high-relief handle, which represents a particular type of weevil. Significantly, the Kuba name for this insect is *ntshyeem,* the same as that of the supreme deity. The motif appears solely on works produced for the divine king and a handful of important nobles. The weevil is one of the few insect types to appear in Kuba arts. Admired for its ability to survive for months at a time with no nourishment, as well as its extremely hard shell, the weevil also appears on important costumes. The actual shell may be worn, or it may be reproduced in metal, sometimes encircled with beads (Cornet 1982, 179). An analogy can be drawn between the insect and the powerful men who exemplify the traits of strength, cunning, and endurance.   PM

Provenance: Alan Brandt, New York

64 CHIEF'S CHAIR

Chokwe, Angola
Wood, hide
85.1 x 33 x 33.7 cm
(33¹/₂ x 13 x 13¹/₄ in.)
Faxon Collection

Finely carved chairs modeled after European prototypes have been made by the Chokwe peoples of Angola and Zaire since the eighteenth century. These chairs, reserved for the use of local chiefs, often included representations of domestic and ritual activities along the backs and splats and occasionally on figurative finials. While all Chokwe men acquire carving skills as part of their education in the *mukanda* initiation rites, it is the professional carvers, or *songi*, who create the beautifully crafted chairs and figures most often found in Western collections.

Although the power of the chiefs has diminished over time, they remain the symbolic center of village life. The chief occupies the place of honor on a veranda in front of his dwelling receiving visitors, hearing disputes, and overseeing all communal activities (Crowley 1972, 31-32). His chair is thus a literal seat of power, serving both to elevate him above his subjects and to locate his authority (Kauenhoven-Janzen 1981, 69). Unfortunately, since most of the decorated chairs have been removed to the West, current chiefs often use imported upholstered or wooden chairs (Crowley 1972, 32).

While the decorative programs of the carved chairs may include scenes from everyday life, when considered as a whole they emerge as carefully planned iconographic statements. This chair, less ornate than many, is nevertheless suggestive of a number of important facets of Chokwe ritual and political organization. The face rendered in high relief on the back represents the *mwana Pwo* (young woman) masks, which are used in both mukanda rites and secular contexts. In an exceptional gesture, the artist has made this identification clear by hollowing out the reverse side. Pwo masks, often modeled after women of exceptional beauty, are symbolic of the female ancestor. Their performance is believed to impart fertility to the spectators (Bastin 1982, 89). Fertility, like abundance of game, is dependent upon the chief, who inherits the sacred power necessary to insure the village's prosperity and well-being from his ancestors. The inclusion of the mwana Pwo mask serves as a potent visual reminder of the king's responsibilities and powers.

The chair's association with mukanda is also significant, for it is the chief who presides over this most important feature of Chokwe life. In their seclusion in the mukanda camp, adolescent boys are educated in all aspects of Chokwe life and culture: hunting, dancing, carving, sexual relations, and traditional beliefs. Several other masks are associated with mukanda, the most important of which is *cikunza*. Distinguished by a tall, cone-shaped headdress representing the horn of a roan antelope, cikunza masks are made of resin-covered barkcloth. Carved wooden representations also appear on chairs and hunters' whistles. Symbolic of the spirit associated with good hunting—the preeminent male activity—the left finial of this chair probably represents cikunza (Bastin 1982, 83).

Unfortunately, the right finial is more difficult to identify. The upswept, bulbous projection from the head of this figure may be a schematic representation of another mask type's headdress or it may represent an ornate plaited hairstyle. The simplistic treatment of the body, like that of the cikunza image, finds parallels in the carved representations of *mahamba* (singular *hamba*) or guardian spirits that serve as intermediaries with the creator god. Because these spirits are not associated with specific individuals, they lack the scarification patterns that are faithfully recorded in the masks and human figures. Freestanding mahamba figures generally have male or female attributes and are usually found in pairs (Bastin 1982, 106). In the absence of anatomical features or clear parallels for the headdress, the right figure's identification as a female hamba is necessarily tentative. If this is correct, then the figure serves both to protect the chief and to remind his subjects of his role as the guardian of the communal mahamba. This conflation of mask and mahamba references in the chief's chair powerfully asserts the traditional role of the ruler as the central focus of spiritual, social, and political life.   PM

Provenance: Alan Brandt, New York

65 NECKLACE

Akan, Ghana
Gold
l. 57.8 cm (22³/₄ in.)
Private Collection

For centuries, the Akan peoples of Ghana have been renowned in the West for their exquisite goldwork. Living in a tropical forest zone with abundant mineral deposits, Akan groups have exploited these precious resources since long before the first Europeans arrived. Contact with Mande traders along the northern edges of Akan lands in the fourteenth century provided an important stimulus for the development of mining, which in turn increased the wealth of a number of Akan city-states. From the Mande, the Akan adopted the use of gold dust as currency based on Arabic weight systems, thus creating the many intriguing gold weights so popular with European and American collectors. Mande influence was also crucial for the development of casting metals, and the earliest Akan examples of goldwork were probably derived from grassland examples (Garrard 1989, 41-42).

With the arrival of the Europeans, the trade in gold increased dramatically. Early travelers' accounts and shipping records indicate that both gold dust and worked gold were traded for European cloth, copper, and other prestige items. These writers inevitably commented on the sumptuous displays of wealth worn by kings and dignitaries at court, including many strands of ornately worked beads similar to these worn about the neck, wrists, and ankles. Unfortunately, despite the impressive artistry of the Akan gold pieces, the Europeans generally melted down the worked pieces for recasting or minting later. Consequently, very few early pieces exist in Western collections.

The recycling of gold was also practiced by the Akan themselves. Because early pieces were created from exceptionally pure metal, they were soft and easily damaged, necessitating frequent recasting (Ehrlich 1989, 53). Oral tradition also states that at the formation of the powerful Asante confederation in 1701, a royal decree was issued requiring that all objects symbolic of the past were to be destroyed, which would surely have included the many pieces of gold jewelry and regalia belonging to the previous court. Finally, a British record of 1817 states that another decree requiring the annual recasting of gold had been issued by the king of the Asante (Garrard 1989, 13).

Despite the frequent recasting of objects, a remarkable stylistic similarity exists between what little early Akan goldwork is known and that of more recent manufacture. A close comparison of the present example, likely cast in the twentieth century, with the drawings created by the seventeenth-century French slave trader Jean Barbot reveals certain continuities (Barbot in Garrard 1989). Both the disc-shaped beads and the diamond-shaped beads formed by adjacent small loops find less elaborate precedents in Barbot's journals, as do some of the smaller ring-shaped and tubular beads. The similarities between these abstract, geometrically patterned beads and certain grasslands examples may support the notion that early Akan goldwork was strongly influenced by examples traded from the Mande. In particular, the beautiful disc-shaped beads, like the well-known soul-washer's discs, may derive either from the beads of the Mali-Senegal region or perhaps from North African coins, which are known to have reached Ghana via the Saharan trade routes (Garrard 1989, 67-68).

A notable divergence occurs, however, in the recent work's inclusion of several gold teeth, seeds, and shells. The casting of objects from nature was noted by early travelers, but appears to have become more commonplace in the nineteenth and twentieth centuries (Ehrlich 1989, 54). Many of these objects have proverbial significance and serve as a means of communication. A necklace was also perceived as providing spiritual or magical protection, for its name, *suman*, means amulets or talismans (Garrard 1989, 226).

The relatively large size of the beads and the more elaborate surface patterning on this example are also typical of later Akan goldwork. The delicate relief apparent on the disc- and shell-shaped beads reveals the hand of a highly skilled artist. It is likely, therefore, that the piece was created in one of the workshops in or around the Asante royal capital of Kumasi, which has been an important center for goldsmithing since the confederation's founding in 1701 (Garrard 1989, 66).   PM

66 CHEVRON BEAD NECKLACE

Cameroon

Glass

l. 45.7 cm (18 in.)

Collection of Dr. Sarah Carolyn Adams Reese

Throughout their history dating as far back as the period between 300 B.C. and A.D. 200, the people of sub-Saharan African have manufactured and imported glass beads. These colorful articles of adornment were important symbols of status and kingship as can be seen on the bronze portraits of the twelfth-century kings of Ife, who generally wear short kilts or sarongs, but are covered with many strands of beads both in semi-precious stones and glass.

When the Portuguese set up trading ports along the west coast of Africa in the fifteenth century, they brought glass beads primarily made in Venice, which must have served as currency and as adornment. Chevron beads (identified by their zigzag patterns) were widely imported in the nineteenth and early twentieth centuries and soon became symbols of kingship in many parts of West Africa, especially among the Bamileke and other people of the Cameroon grasslands.   MK

(67) BEAD NECKLACE

Mali and Niger
Amber
l. 54 cm (21¼ in.)
Collection of Dr. Sarah Carolyn Adams Reese

Throughout sub-Saharan Africa, necklaces of beads have much more significance to the wearer than mere ornaments. On most occasions, beads are badges that confer social and political status on the people who wear them. For instance, in Benin the wearing of coral beads was reserved for the oba and his immediate family and was an essential emblem of his office (Ben-Amos 1980, 20). Similarly, necklaces composed primarily of certain highly prized beads were emblems of kingship among the Luba and would be circulated only among kings, chiefs, and other title holders (Roberts and Roberts 1996, 94).

Frequently, necklaces were composed of semi-precious stones and other materials of high intrinsic value imported from distant places. Magnificent amber beads such as these were worn primarily by the West African nomadic populations such as the Fulani in Mali and Niger. Amber beads from Africa may be softer than European amber from the Baltic shores but they are also highly prized by their owners. In Fulani culture women wear large amber beaded necklaces or headbands as indicators of their marital status and material wealth. MK

⑥⑧ SPOON WITH FEMALE FIGURE

Kwale Ibo, Nigeria

Wood

h. 55.3 cm (21³/₄ in.)

Collection of

Dr. Robert E. L. Perkins

The Ibo-speaking peoples of eastern Nigeria form a loosely related cultural group with distinctive regional artistic traditions. This spoon has been identified with the Kwale Ibo in the far western reaches of Ibo lands, which are surrounded by various Edo-speaking sub-groups. Historically, the Kwale Ibo were occasionally under the political domination of the Edo rulers of the Benin Kingdom (G. I. Jones 1984, 146). Throughout the Niger and Cross River delta regions, the various ethnic groups have experienced often profound cultural exchanges, as witnessed by their related languages and their many shared religious and social structures.

Although several excellent studies have been conducted on the central, northern, and eastern Ibo, the western groups have received little attention. The few definitely attributed western Ibo pieces in museums were largely collected in the nineteenth century, and these were mostly from groups living further south than the Kwale (G. I. Jones 1984, 146-47). The British anthropologist G. I. Jones has published a Kwale recumbent male figure that was used as a headpiece in the *Ekeleke* masquerade (G. I. Jones 1984, fig. 56). While it differs from this piece in the treatment of the body, which is proportionally smaller and has a broader chest, the facial treatment is remarkably similar. In both, the eyes are reduced to narrow slits beneath arched brows, and the wide, straight mouth features filed teeth. Characteristic of western Ibo sculpture is the inclusion of long parallel lines arranged across a broad forehead. Faint traces of these marks are visible on this spoon figure, representing the scarification patterns that formerly distinguished the inhabitants of the region (G. I. Jones 1989, 47-48).

The original purpose for this piece is uncertain. In the far eastern regions inhabited by the Cross River Ibo, spoons, or more properly, bowls with single handles in the form of a female figure, are used to offer white chalk in hospitality ceremonies. Associated with purity, regeneration, honesty, and spiritual sacrifices, chalk is frequently offered to important guests and participants in certain rituals (Cole 1991, 50-51). Chalk also had protective properties and was given to strangers who were safeguarded by influential village men. After marking

their wrists or hands with two lines, the visitors would return the chalk to the bowl (G. I. Jones 1984, 121).

It seems unlikely, however, that this spoon served the same functions as the eastern chalk spoons. Clearly chalk is important in western Ibo culture, as it also is among their Edo neighbors, but the structural differences between this piece and Cross River examples are striking enough to suggest an alternative purpose. The curved bowl and significantly longer handle differ markedly, as does the strongly vertical emphasis of the composition. Furthermore, those Cross River examples that include figures have them oriented so that the recipient views the upright figure. Finally, eastern chalk servers are frequently polychromed, but this piece shows no traces of pigment.

In Nsukka, in the far northern reaches of Ibo lands, certain important women own finely ornamented spoons. Carved for the title-taking rites of those who have reached an elevated level in the women's association, these spoons are carried by a young female attendant who accompanies the owner on a ceremonial walk through the market. This status symbol attracts the attention of the villagers, who give gifts to the senior woman in celebration of her new status. The owner also brings the object to her association meetings (Cole and Aniakor 1984, 54).

Unfortunately, it is not clear whether this spoon may have been intended for similar purposes. Certainly the orientation of the figure relative to the handle suggests a display purpose, as the figure would stand erect if the handle were grasped. In addition, the small bands indicated beneath the knees of the figure, which abruptly terminate in the handle, may represent the long ivory leglets worn by titled women in many Ibo groups. At over twenty-one inches in height, the size of this work compares favorably with published Nsukka title-spoons. However, until more extensive studies of the art and social structures of the western Ibo are conducted, the exact purpose of this work will remain a mystery.   PM

Provenance: Eric Robertson, New York

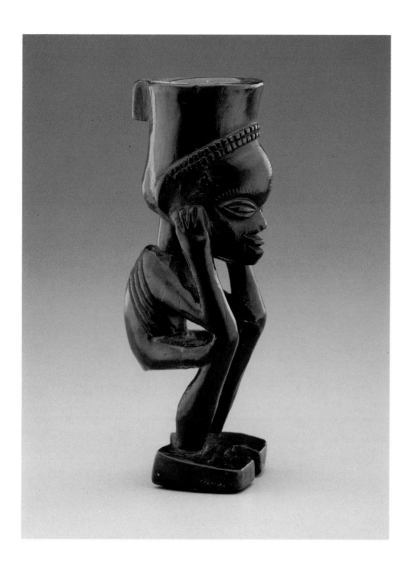

69 TOBACCO MORTAR

Bena Lulua, Zaire
Wood
h. 4 ³/₄ in. (12.1 cm)
The Collection of Laura
and James Sherman

Small figural mortars used for grinding and carrying snuff were carved by many groups in the Angola-Zaire region, including the Bena Lulua, Chokwe, and Luba peoples. The wide dispersion of the form attests both to the extensive trade in tobacco and the significant cultural interchange between these groups in the past. While these groups shared certain cultural features, they differed in others, and it is only in recent decades that a broader group identification has emerged. Their early heterogeneity is clearly noticeable in their many sculptures, which also demonstrate the influences of several neighboring groups like the Kete, Luba, Chokwe, and Songye.

Like this little mortar figure, most Lulua works display a 1:4 head-to-body ratio, often with a pointed hair style. The neck is generally long and thin, the shoulders curved and scarified or tattooed, the arms positioned at right angles to the torso, and the relatively short legs culminating in very large, bare feet (Timmermans 1966, 18). Facial features are carefully delineated and usually show both an upper and lower eyelid and a slightly upturned mouth.

The crouching pose of this figure is frequently employed for mortars and appears occasionally in other types of Lulua sculptures. It is, however, extremely rare in the arts of other African peoples (Roy 1992, 151). The beautiful oppositions of line formed by the bent elbows resting upon bent knees creates a precariousness counterbalanced by the enlarged head and feet. Many different interpretations have been offered for this distinctive pose, including identifications as guardians, hunters, or chiefs (Timmermans 1966, 26).

It has been suggested that the crouching mortars were likely owned by hunters, as the straps that are often attached to the heads would have allowed the pieces to be affixed to a belt. Since many examples are lidded, they would have served as both mortar and container. The pose might then mimic the hunter's, when he squats to smoke before tracking his prey (Timmermans 1966, 27).

In his description of a similar piece in the Stanley Collection, Christopher Roy notes that the emaciation, enlarged head, and unsettling stare may represent the effects of hemp smoking (Roy 1992, 151). The practice of smoking marijuana had been introduced under the reign of Kalamba Mukenga, a nineteenth-century chief of the Bashilange peoples of the middle Lulua river basin. According to a tradition recorded by a German explorer, Kalamba Mukenga, at the urging of his sister, had instituted the cult of Riamba, whose central practice was the smoking of hemp at all ceremonial and political events. As a demonstration of a break with the past, the chief demanded that the people destroy all of their sculptural figures, which were believed to contain important magical powers. The Riamba cult eventually spread to other peoples, and is now blamed for the loss of a tremendous amount of early Zairian art (Maes 1939, 7539-41).

It has further been suggested that sculptures were then remade in honor of the chief with artists working wholly for the cult of Riamba. The mortars may date from this period and would therefore be intended for the use of hemp rather than tobacco (Maes 1939, 7542). If this theory is correct, then the pose and expression of these figures may well reflect the effects of hemp smoking. The mortars would thus be endowed with a socio-religious significance, referring to this most central practice of the new religion. PM

Provenance: Donald Morris Gallery, Birmingham, Michigan

70 HELMET MASK

Igala, Nigeria
Wood, pigment
h. 30.5 cm (12 in.)
The Detroit Institute of Arts
Founders Society Purchase
with funds from Margaret
H. Demant, Dede and
Oscar Feldman, Robert
Jacobs, and Ellen and
William Kahn in honor of
Michael Kan (1996.16)

The Igala of Nigeria are closely related linguistically and culturally to the Yoruba peoples. Their history dates to the sixteenth and seventeenth centuries, when they were conquered and made part of the Benin kingdom, then at the height of its power. A number of Benin bronze plaques from this period commemorate the wars of conquest launched by the Benin oba against the *ata*, or king, of Idah, ruler of the Igala people.

Helmet masks such as this, which completely cover the wearer's head, closely resemble in form classic Yoruba carvings such as the Gelede mask. The magnificent Detroit sculpture demonstrates the facial striations reminiscent of Ife royal portraiture of the twelfth and fifteenth centuries.

Wooden helmet masks, first published in the 1940s, are almost identical in style to this example, except for their headdresses covered with red and black abrus seeds. They appeared in public during the Ojo festival in March and the Egu festival in September and seem to be associated with ceremonies celebrating the founding of the royal lineage (Sieber and Walker 1987). MK

71 COMB WITH KNEELING FEMALE FIGURE

Luba, Zaire
Wood
h. 15.2 cm (6 in.)
The Collection of
Joyce Marie Sims

The Luba perceive both spiritual and physical beauty as cultivated attributes that are achieved through corporal transformations and elegant hairdressing. Finely carved combs are used to create the elaborate hair styles signifying profession, status, title, and personal history. Like ornate scarification, beautiful coiffures were a mark of civilized refinement that indicated the moral worth of an individual (Nooter Roberts and Roberts 1996, fig. 9). The female figure depicted here, with plaited hair style and elongated genitals, embodies these qualities.

This image embodies the physical alterations that are required for spirit mediumship, divination, and membership in the *Budye* society (Nooter 1991, passim). Holding her breasts, which are said to hide the secrets of sacred kingship, the figure refers to the unique ability of women to communicate with the ancestral realm.   PM

Provenance: Peter Boyd, Indiana

72 LINGUIST STAFF

Akan, Ghana
Wood, pigment, gold leaf
h. 160 cm (63 in.)
The Collection of
Albert Nuamah

The Akan peoples of the forest region of Ghana and Côte d'Ivoire are known for their centralized political structures. Organized around matrilineages, the Akan live in communities ranging from villages of a few score of people to large towns of thousands, each ruled by a head-man (*odikro*) or chief (*ohene*) in whom resides the authority over the economic and ritual life of the community. The Akan chief presides over a court and a bureaucracy composed of officials, both royal and non-royal, who are ranked hierarchically. Of the many non-royal offices in a chiefdom, the position of the linguist (*okyeame*) is the most respected. European visitors to the Ghanaian coast were quick to notice the essential role played by this courtier as early as the seventeenth century. They also noted that the linguist was not only the spokes-person of the chief but also an advisor, an intermediary with his subjects, a store of knowledge, a legal expert, an ambassador, and occasionally, a ritual officiator.

In Akan culture, various emblems are known to distinguish state officials. For the traditional linguist, a staff (*okyeame poma*), similar to this piece, constitutes the principal symbol that both marks his office and facili-tates his functions in and out of court. The linguist staff is often a carved wooden shaft, frequently segmented and assembled from three parts: a spiked base, a midsection, and a figurative finial. The shaft is frequently painted either black, gold, or silver over a chip-carved or incised surface. The finial has on it an animal, plant, human figure, or artifact, or a combination of these. Considered critical to the political signifi-cance of the staff, the figurative motif is usually gilded for visual effect. Gold repre-sents social prestige and material wealth in Akan culture, and its use in gilding this piece would have thus said a lot about the economic position of its owner.

The staff would have been carried by the linguist when the chief was sitting in court or to herald the ruler's arrival at a public gathering. In Akan culture, visual forms tend to have direct verbal equivalents, an interconnection that is brought out more powerfully in linguist staff imagery than anywhere elsewhere. At the highest levels of political discourse, the art of speaking is considered the domain of the traditional linguist. A competent okyeame must be articulate, eloquent, and concise in inter-preting the ruler's thoughts and traditional lore in a clear and assertive manner. In particular, he must be adept at proverbial language because, in a traditional chief's court, there is hardly any serious conversa-tion that does not use proverbs and sayings.

Hundreds of proverbs are known and used by the Akan people, but there are some that reflect on political authority either because they best distill power rela-tionships or convey the virtues of leadership. This staff's iconography is uniquely suited for the purpose; its symbolism communicates ideas about the chief and his rule. Its imagery is designed to make a poignant, thought-provoking statement deemed relevant for the occasion. For example, this staff has a carved finial of a pot with a ram's head atop, set on a traditional hearth. Like most linguist staffs, the imagery depicts an Akan proverb: "Aboa tiri enyera nkwan mu" or "An animal's head is never lost in a soup." Like the prominent animal head, the ruler is the dominant focus of Akan society.

Linguist staffs are believed to be based on European prototypes introduced in the nineteenth century (Mcleod 1980). Unlike its precursors which were decorated with cast silver motifs, the Akan type emphasizes gold as its most appropriate medium.   NQ

CATALOGUE AUTHORS

LBH	Laura Bassett Ho
MK	Michael Kan
MLW	Michelle Lee White
ON	Odetta Norton
PM	Pamela Pillsbury McKee
NQ	Nii Otokunor Quarcoopome
DR	Daniel Ramirez
LR	Lisa Roberts
TS	Trevor Schoonmaker
CTM	Chie Tashima McKenney
RV	Roberto Visani

AFRICAN FORM AND IMAGERY

BIBLIOGRAPHY

Abimbola, Wande
1977   *Ifa Divination Poetry*. New York: NOK Publishers.

1994   "Ifa: A West African Cosmological System." In *Religion in Africa: Experience & Expression*, Monograph Series of the David M. Kennedy Center for International Studies at Brigham Young University, ed. Thomas D.Blakely, Walter E. A. van Beek, and Dennis L. Thomson, vol. IV. Provo, Utah.

Abiodun, Rowland
1983   "Identity and the Artistic Process in the Yoruba Concept of Iwa." *Journal of Cultures and Ideas* 1:13-30.

1987   "Verbal and Visual Metaphors: Mythical Allusions in Yoruba Realistic Art of Ori." *Word and Image* 3 (3): 252-70.

Adams, Monni
1978   "Kuba Embroidered Cloth." *African Arts* 12 (1): 24-39, 106-7.

1988   "Eighteenth century Kuba King Figures." *African Arts* 21 (3): 32-38.

Adamson, Joy
1967   *The Peoples of Kenya*. New York: Harcourt, Brace and World.

Agwuna, Igwe Osita
1984   "Ikenga Defined in Terms of Form and Concept." *Ikoro* 5 (1-2): 53-71.

Akpan, Joseph J.
1994   "Ekpo Society Masks of the Ibo." *African Arts* 27 (4): 48-53.

Alldridge, F. R. G. S.
1901   *The Sharbro and Its Hinterland*. London: Macmillan and Co.

Amick, Joan, ed.
1995   *Art from the Forge*. Washington, D.C.: National Museum of African Art.

Aniakor, Chike
1973   "Structuralism in Ikenga: An Ethnoaesthetic Approach." *Ikenga* 2 (1): 6-28.

Antiri, Janet Adwoa
1974   "Akan Combs." *African Arts* 8 (1): 32-35.

Anyika, F.
1988   "The Chi Concept in Igbo Religious Thought." *Africana Marburgensia* 21 (2): 40-50.

Armstrong, Robert Plant
1983   "Oshe-Shango and the Dynamic of Doubling." *African Arts* Feb: 28-33.

Arnheim, Rudolf
1992   *To the Rescue of Art: Twenty-Six Essays*. Berkeley and Los Angeles: University of California Press.

Arnoldi, Mary Jo, and Christine Mullen Kraemer
1995   *Crowning Achievements: African Arts of Dressing the Head*. University of California, Los Angeles: Fowler Museum of Cultural History.

Aronson, Lisa
1992   "The Language of West African Textiles." *African Art* 25: 36-40.

Bascom, William
1969   *Ifa Divination: Communication Between Gods and Men in West Africa*. Bloomington: Indiana University Press.

1973   *African Art in Cultural Perspective*. New York: W. W. Norton and Co.

Bastin, Marie-Louise
1982   *La Sculpture Ishokwe*. trans. J. B. Donne. Meudon, France: Alain et Françoise Chaffin.

1984   "Ritual Masks of the Chokwe." *African Arts* 17:4 (August): 0-45, 92-93, 95-96.

1992   "The Mwanangana Chokwe Chief and Art (Angola)." In *Kings of Africa: Art and Authority in Africa.*, ed. Erna Beumers and Hans-Joachim Koloss. Utrecht: 65-70.

Beier, Ulli
1970   *Yoruba Poetry: An Anthology of Traditional Poems*. London: Cambridge University Press.

Ben-Amos, Paula

1980　*The Art of Benin*. London: Thames and Hudson.

1984　"Men and Animals in Benin Art." *Man* 11: 243-52.

1991　"Carvings and Castings Are Our Olden Days Photographs: Art and History in the Benin Kingdom, Nigeria." *Arts d'Afrique Noire* 80 (Winter): 29-42.

Ben-Amos, Paula, and Arnold Rubin, eds.

1985　*Art of Power, Power of Art: Studies in Benin Kingship Iconography*. Los Angeles: UCLA Museum of Cultural History, University of California, Monograph Series, no. 19, exh. cat.

Bentor, Eli

1988　"Life as an Artistic Process: Igbo Ikenga and Ofo." *African Arts* 21 (2): 66-71.

Bernus, Edmond

1984　*Les Touaregs Pasteurs et guerriers des sables*. Paris: Editions de l'Office de la recherche scientifique et technique outre-mer.

Beumers, Erna, and Hans-Joachim Koloss, eds.

1992　*Kings of Africa*. Maastricht, the Netherlands: MECC, exh. cat.

Biebuyck, Daniel

1973　*Lega Culture: Art, Initiation, and Moral Philosophy Among a Central African People*. Berkeley: University of California Press.

1985　*The Arts of Zaire*. vol.1. Berkeley and Los Angeles: University of California Press.

1986　*The Arts of Zaire*. vol.2. Berkeley and Los Angeles: University of California Press.

1987　*The Arts of Central Africa*. Boston, Mass: G.K. Hall.

1989　*Power of Headdresses: A Cross-cultural Study of Forms and Functions*. Brussels: Tendi S.A.

Binkley, David

1987　"Avatar of Power: Southern Kuba Masquerade figures in a funerary context." *Africa* 57 (1): 75-97.

1990　In *Art of Central Africa: Masterpieces from the Berlin Museum für Völkerunde*. pp.46-7, New York: The Metropolitan Museum of Art.

Blackmun, Barbara Winston

1991　"The Face of the Leopard: Its Significance in Benin Court Art." In *Allen Memorial Art Museum Bulletin* (Oberlin College), 44 (2): 24-32.

Blakely, Thomas D., and Pamela A. R. Blakely

1987　"So'o Masks and Hemba Funerary Festival." *African Arts* 21 (1): 30-37, 84-86.

n.d.　"Ancestors, Witchcraft, and Foregrounding the Poetic: Men's Oratory and Women's Song-Dance in Hemba Funerary Performance."

Blier, Suzanne Preston

1976　*Beauty and the Beast: A Study in Contrasts*. 4 Nov.-31 Dec. New York: Tribal Arts Gallery Two, exh. cat.

Boone, Sylvia A.

1986　*Radiance from the Waters: Ideals of Feminine Beauty in Mende Art*. New Haven: Yale University Press.

Borgatti, Jean M.

1990　"Portraiture in Africa." *African Arts* 23: 3-4.

Boston, John

1977　*Ikenga Figures among the North-west Igbo and the Igala*. Nigeria: Ethnographia and The Federal Department of Antiquities.

Bourgeois, Arthur, P.

1979　*Nkanda related sculpture of the Yaka and Suku of southwestern Zaire*. Bloomington: Indiana University Press

1981　"Helmet-shaped Masks of the Suku and Their Neighbors." *Arts d'Afrique Noire* 39: 26-41.

1984　*Art of the Yaka and the Suku*. trans. J. B. Donne. Meudon, France: Alain et François Chaffin.

1995　"Figurative Pipes of the Kwango Region of Zaire." *Arts d'Afrique Noire* 94: 17-26.

Bradbury, R. E.

1973　*Benin Studies*. London: Oxford University Press for the International African Institute.

Brain, Robert, and Adam Pollock

1971　*Bangwa Funerary Sculpture*. London: Duckworth.

Bravmann, Réné

1973　*Open Frontiers: The Mobility of Art in Africa*. Seattle: University of Washington Press, Index of Art in the Pacific Northwest, no. 5, exh. cat.

Brincard, Marie-Therese

1989　*Sounding Forms: African Musical Instruments*. New York: National Museum of African Art.

Buckley, Anthony D.

1985　*Yoruba Medicine*. London: Clarendon Press.

Casajus, Dominique

1985　*Peau d'Éne et autres contes Touaregs*. Paris: Editions L'Harmattan.

1987　*La tente dans la solitude: La societe et les morts chez les Touaregs Kel Ferwan*. Cambridge: Cambridge University Press.

Casti, Gaetano

1891　*Ten Years in Equatoria and the Return with Emin Pasha*. 2 vols. London: Frederick Warne.

Celenko, Theodore
1983   *A Treasury of African Art from the Harrison Eiteljorg Collection.* Bloomington: Indiana University Press.

Ceyssens, Rik
1993   "Material and Formal Aspects of Masks from the Upper Kasai." In *Face of the Spirits: Masks of the Zaire Basin,* ed. Frank Herreman and Constantin Petridis. Antwerp: Ethnographic Museum, and Washington: Smithsonian Institution, exh. cat.

Cole, Herbert M.
1977   *The Arts of Ghana.* Los Angeles: Museum of Cultural History, University of California, exh. cat.

1984   "Igbo Arts at UCLA." *African Arts* 18 (1): 64-68.

1988   "Igbo Arts and Ethnicity: Problems and Issues." *African Arts* 21 (2): 26-27.

1989   *Icons: Ideals and Power in the Art of Africa.* Washington, D.C.: National Museum of African Art, exh. cat.

1991   "Igbo Chalk Vessels." In *Spoons in African Art,* ed. Lorenz Homberger. Zurich: Museum Rietberg, exh. cat.

Cole, Herbert M., ed.
1985   *I Am Not Myself: The Art of African Masquerade.* Los Angeles: University of California.

Cole, Herbert M., and Chike C. Aniakor
1984   *Igbo Arts: Community and Cosmos.* Los Angeles: Museum of Cultural History, University of California, exh. cat.

Consentino, Donald
1987   "Who Is That Fellow in the Many-Colored Cap? Transformations of Eshu in Old and New World Mythologies." *Journal of American Folklore* 100: 261-275.

Cornet, Joseph
1971   *Art of Africa: Treasures from the Congo.,* trans. Barbara Thompson. London: Phaidon Press.

1975   *Art from Zaire: 100 Masterworks from the National Collection; L'Art du Zaire: An Exhibition of Traditional Art from the Institute of National Museums of Zaire,* trans. Irwin Hersey. New York: African-American Institute, exh. cat.

1978   *A Survey of Zairian Art: The Bronson Collection.* Raleigh: The North Carolina Museum of Art, exh. cat.

1982   *Art Royal Kuba.* Milan: Edizione Sipiel.

1994   "Masks among the Kuba Peoples." In *Face of the Spirits: Masks from the Zaire Basin,* ed. Frank Herreman and Constantin Petridis. Antwerp: Ethnographic Museum, and Washington: Smithsonian Institution, exh. cat. pp. 129-42.

Crowley, Daniel J.
1972   "Chokwe: Political Art in a Plebian Society." In *African Art and Leadership.,* ed. Douglas Fraser and Herbert M. Cole., Madison: University of Wisconsin Press.

Dark, Philip
1973   *An Introduction to Benin Art and Technology.* Oxford: Clarendon.

Dewey, William J.
1993   *Sleeping Beauties: The Jerome L. Joss Collection of African Headrests at University of California Los Angeles*: University of California Los Angeles/Fowler Museum of Cultural History, exh. cat.

Domowitz, Susan
1992   "Wearing Proverbs: Anyi Names for Printed Factory Cloth." *African Arts* 25: 82-87.

Drewal, Henry John
1977   *Traditional Art of the Nigerian Peoples: The Milton D. Ratner Family Collection.* Washington, D.C.: National Museum of African Art, exh. cat.

1988   "Beauty and Being: Aesthetics and Ontology in Yoruba Body Art." In *Marks of Civilization: Artistic Transformations of the Human Body,* ed. Arnold Rubin. Los Angeles: Museum of Cultural History, University of California.

Drewal, Henry John, and Margaret Thompson Drewal
1975   "Gelede Dance of the Western Yoruba." *African Arts* 8(2): 36-45.

1983   *Gelede: Art and Female Power among the Yoruba.* Bloomington: Indiana University Press.

Drewal, Henry John, and John Pemberton III with Rowland Abiodun
1989   *Yoruba: Nine Centuries of African Art and Thought,* ed. Allen Wardwell. New York: Center for African Art, exh. cat.

1994   *The Yoruba Artist: New Theoretical Perspectives on African Arts.* Washington, D.C.: Smithsonian Institution Press.

Drewal, Margaret Thompson
1977   "Projections from the Top in Yoruba Art." *African Arts* 11 (1): 43-49, 91-92.

1986   "Art and Trance among Yoruba Shango Devotees." *African Arts* 20 (1): 60-67.

Duchâteau, Armand
1994   *Benin: Royal Art of Africa from the Museum für Völkerkunde, Vienna.* Houston: Museum of Fine Arts, exh. cat.

Ehrlich, Martha J.
1989   "Early Akan Gold from the Wreck of the Whydah." *African Arts* 22 (4): 52-57, 87-88.

Eyo, Ekpo and Frank Willett
1980   *Treasures of Ancient Nigeria.* New York: Alfred A. Knopf.

Ezra, Kate

1983   *Figure Sculpture of the Bamana of Mali.* Ann Arbor: University Microfilms.

1986   *A Human Ideal in African Art: Bamana Figurative Sculpture.* Washington, D.C.: National Museum of African Art, exh. cat.

1988   *Art of the Dogon (Selections from the Lester Wunderman Collection).* New York: The Metropolitan Museum of Art, exh. cat.

1992   *Royal Art of Benin: The Perls Collection in the Metropolitan Museum of Art.* New York: The Metropolitan Museum of Art, exh. cat.

Fagaly, William

1989   *Shapes of Power, Belief, and Celebration: African Art from New Orleans Collections.* New Orleans: New Orleans Museum of Art, exh. cat.

Fagg, William

1965   *Tribes and Forms in African Art.* New York: Tudor.

1968   *African Tribal Images: The Katherine White Reswick Collection.* Cleveland: The Cleveland Museum of Art.

1970   *African Sculpture.* Washington, D.C.: International Exhibition Foundation, exh. cat.

1970   *The Tribal Image.* London: British Museum.

1980   *Yoruba Beadwork: Art of Nigeria.* New York: Rizzoli International Publishers for Pace Gallery.

1982   *Yoruba: Sculpture of West Africa.* New York: Alfred A. Knopf.

1990   commentary in *The Harry A. Franklin Family Collection of African Art,* Sotheby's, New York, April 4.

Felix, Marc L.

1987   *100 Peoples of Zaire and their Sculpture: The Handbook.* Brussels: Zaire Basin Art History Research Foundation.

1990   *Mwana hiti: Life and Art of the Matrilineal Bantu of Tanzania.* Munich: Verlag Fred Jahn.

Fernandez, James W.

1966   "Principles of Vitality and Opposition in Fang Aesthetics." *The Journal of Aesthetics and Art Criticism* 25(1): 53-64.

1982   *Bwiti: An Ethnography of the Religious Imagination in Africa.* Princeton: Princeton University Press.

Fischer, Eberhard, and Hans Himmelheber

1984   *The Arts of the Dan in West Africa.,* trans. Anne Biddle, ed. Susan Curtis. Zurich: Museum Rietberg, exh. cat. (org. pub. *Die Kunst der Dan,* 1976).

Flam, Jack D.

1971   "The Symbolic Structure of Baluba Caryatid Stools." *African Arts* 4 (2): 55-59, 80.

Forde, Daryll, and Jones, G. I.

1950   *The Ibo and Ibibio-speaking Peoples of Southeastern Nigeria.* London: Published for the International African Institute.

Forde, Daryll, et al.

1962   *Essays on the Ritual of Social Relations.,* ed. Max Gluckman. Manchester, England: Manchester University Press.

Fortes, Meyer

1962   *Marriage in Tribal Societies.* Cambridge, England: Published for the Department of Archaeology and Anthropology at the University Press.

Frank, Barbara

1987   "Open Borders: Style and Ethnic Identity." *African Arts* 20 (4): 48-55.

Freyer, Bryna

1987   *Royal Benin Art in the Collection of the National Museum of African Art.* Washington, D.C.: Published for the National Museum of African Art by the Smithsonian Institution Press.

Gabus, Jean

1982   *Sahara, bijoux et techniques.* Neuchâtel: A la Baconniere.

Garrard, Timothy F.

1989   *Gold of Africa: Jewellery and Ornaments from Ghana, Côte d'Ivoire, Mali, and Senegal in the Collection of the Barbier-Mueller Museum.* Munich: Prestel.

Gebauer, Paul

1971   "Art of Cameroon." *African Arts* 4 (2): 24-35.

1979   *Art of Cameroon.* Portland, Oregon: The Portland Museum of Art, exh. cat.

Georgia Museum of Art

1990   *Art of the Cameroon: Selections from the Spelman College Collection of African Art.* Athens, Georgia: Georgia Museum of Art, exh. cat.

Gilfoy, Peggy S.

1976   *African Art from the Harrison Eiteljorg Collection.* Indianapolis: Indianapolis Museum of Art.

Goldwater, Robert

1960   *Bambara Sculptures from the Western Sudan.* New York: The Museum of Primitive Art.

Goody, Jack

1971   *Technology, Tradition, and the State.* London: Oxford University Press.

Gottschalk, Burkhard

1994   "BUNDU Bush Devils in the Land of the Mende." *African Arts* 27: 20.

Greenberg, Joseph
1963   *Languages of Africa*. Bloomington: Indiana University Press.

Griaule, Marcel, and Germaine Dieterlen
1965   *Le renard pale*. Paris: Institut d'ethnologie.

Handwerker, W. P.
1973   "Technology and Household Configuration in Urban Africa: The Bassa of Monrovia." *American Sociological Review* 38: 182-97.

Harley, George W.
1950   *Masks as Agents of Social Control in Northeast Liberia*. Cambridge, Mass.: Peabody Museum, Papers of the Peabody Museum of American Archaeology and Ethnology, Harvard University, 32 (2).

Harter, Pierre
1990   "Royal Commemorative Figures in the Cameroon Grasslands: Ateu Atsa, a Bangwa Artist." *African Arts* 23 (4): 70-77.

Herreman, Frank, and Constantin Petridis
1993   *Face of the Spirits: Masks From the Zaire Basin*. Antwerp: Ethnographic Museum, and Washington, D.C.: Smithsonian Institution, exh. cat.

Hersak, Dunja
1985   *Songye Masks and Figure Sculpture*. London: Ethnographica.

Himmelheber, Hans
1964   *Sculptors and Sculptures of the Dan*, ed. L. Brown and M. Crowder. Proceedings of the First International Congress of Africanists. Evanston, Ill.: Northwestern University Press.

Himmelheber, Hans, and Lorenz Homberger
1984   *The Arts of the Dan in West Africa*. Zurich: Rietberg Museum.

Holas, Bernard
1960   *Cultures materialles de la Côte d'Ivoire*. Paris.

Horton, Robin
1965   *Kalabari Sculpture*. Lagos, Nigeria: Federal Department of Antiquities, Nigeria.

Houlberg, Marilyn
1978   "Notes on the Egungun Masquerades among the Oyo Yoruba." *African Arts* 11 (3): 20-27.

Idowu, Bolaji E.
1962   *Olodumare: God in Yoruba Belief*. London: Longmans.

Ikenga-Metuh, Emifie
1983   "A Study of Religion and Art in Igbo Culture." *Orita (Ibidan)* 15 (2): 71-86.

Imperato, Pascal James
1970   "The Dance of the Tyi Wara." *African Arts* 4 (1): 8-13, 71-80.

1980   "Bambara and Malinke Ton Masquerades." *African Arts* 13 (4): 47-55, 82-85, 87.

1983   *Buffoons, Queens and Wooden Horsemen: Dyo and Gouan Societies of the Bambara of Mali*. Manhasset, New York: Kilima House Publishers.

Isola, A.
1976   "The Artistic Aspects of The Sango Pipe." *Odu* 13: 80-103.

Johnson, Barbara
1986   *Four Dan Sculptors: Continuity and Change*. San Francisco: Fine Arts Museum of San Francisco.

Jones, David
1988   *Poets with Adzes: An Introduction to Yoruba Religious Art*. Ipswich, England: Ipswich Borough Council.

Jones, G. I.
1984   *The Art of Eastern Nigeria*. Cambridge: Cambridge University Press.

1989   *Ibo Art*. Aylesbury, England: Shire Ethnography #13.

Kan, Michael and Roy Sieber
1995   *African Masterworks in the Collection of the Detroit Institute of Arts*. Washington, D.C.: The Smithsonian Institution Press.

Kasfir, Sidney Littlefield
1984   "One Tribe-One Style." *History in Africa* 11: 163-193.

Kauenhoven-Janzen, Reinhild
1981   "Chokwe Thrones." *African Arts* 14 (3): 69-74, 92.

Kecskési, Maria
1987   *African Masterpieces and Selected Works from Munich: The Staatliches Museum für Völkerkunde*. New York: The Center for African Art, exh. cat.

Kjersmeier, Carl
1935   *Centres de Style de la Sculpture Negre Africaine*, vol. 1, Paris: Editions Albert Morance.

Knappert, Jan
1987   *East Africa: Kenya, Tanzania and Uganda*. London: Sangam Books Ltd.

Koloss, Hans-Joachim
1990   *Art of Central Africa: Masterpieces from the Berlin Museum für Völkerkunde*. New York: The Metropolitan Museum of Art, exh. cat.

Lamp, Frederick
1986   "The Art of the Baga: A Preliminary Inquiry." *African Arts* 19 (2): 64-67, 92.

1995   Telephone conversation with author, 16 November.

Leloup, Helene

1988   "Dogon Figure Styles." *African Arts* 22(1): 44-51, 98-99.

1994   *Dogon Statuary*. trans. Brunhilde Biebuyck and Daniele Amez. Strasbourg, France: D. Amez.

Leuzinger, Elsy

1978   *Afrikansiche Skulpturen*. Zurich: Rietberg Museum.

MacGaffey, Janet

1975   "Two Kongo Potters." *African Arts* 9 (1): 29-31.

MacGaffey, Wyatt

1977   "Fetishism Revisited: Kongo Nkisi in Sociological Perspective." *Africa* 47 (2): 172-84.

1988   "Complexity, Astonishment, and Power: The Visual Vocabulary of Minkisi." *Journal of South African Studies* 14 (2): 188-203.

1990   "The Personhood of Ritual Objects: Kongo Minkisi." *Etnofoor* 3 (1): 45-61.

1990   Catalogue entry in *Art of Central Africa: Master pieces from the Berlin Museum für Völkerkunde*. New York: The Metropolitan Museum of Art., exh. cat.

MacGaffey, Wyatt, and M. D. Harris

1993   *Astonishment and Power*. Washington, D.C.: The Smithsonian Institution Press.

McKesson, John A., III.

1982   "Ovulation of Fang Reliquary Sculpture." M.A. thesis, Columbia University.

McLeod, Malcolm D.

1980   *Treasures of African Art*. New York: Abbeville Press.

McNaughton, Patrick R.

1970   "The Throwing Knife in African History." *African Arts* (3): 3.

1979   *Secret Sculptures of the Komo: Art and Power in Bamana (Bambara) Initiation Associations*. Philadelphia: Institute for the Study of Human Issues., Working Papers in Traditional Arts 4.

1988   *The Mande Blacksmiths: Knowledge, Power, and Art in West Africa*. Bloomington: Indiana University Press.

1995   In *Africa: The Art of a Continent*, ed. Tom Phillips. London: Royal Academy of Arts.

Maes, Joseph

1939   "Kalamba Mukenga: fondateur du 'Riamba' ou culte du chanvre." *L'Illustration congolaise* 217: 7539-42.

Maurer, Evan M., and Allen F. Roberts

1985   *Tabwa: The Rising of a New Moon: A Century of Tabwa Art*. Ann Arbor, Mich: The University of Michigan Museum of Art, exh. cat.

Mbiti, John

1991   *Introduction to African Religion*. 2nd ed. Ibadan, Nigeria: Heinemann.

Meneghini, Mario

1972   "The Bassa Mask." *African Arts* 6 (1): 44-48.

Merriam, Alan P.

1975   *Culture History of the Basongye*. Bloomington: Indiana University African Studies Program.

1978   "Kifwebe and Other Masked and Unmasked Societies among the Basongye." *Africa-Tervuren* 24 (3) and (4).

Mestach, Jean Willy

1985   *Songe Studies: Form and Symbolism*. Munich: Galerie Jahn.

Messenger, John C.

1973   "The Carver in Anang Society." In *The Traditional Artist in African Societies*, ed. Warren L. d'Azevedo, Bloomington: Indiana University Press.

Meyer, Laure

1995   *Art and Craft in Africa: Everyday Life, Ritual, Court Art*. Paris: Terrail.

Mickelsen, Nancy R.

1976   "Tuareg Jewelry." *African Arts* 9 (2): 16-19.

Murray, Kenneth

1949   "Idah Masks." *Nigerian Field* 14 (3): 85-92.

New York

1979   The African-American Institute. *Traditional Sculpture from Upper Volta: An Exhibition of Objects from New York Museums and Private Collections*. New York: The African-American Institute, exh. cat.

Neyt, François

1981   *Traditional Arts and History of Zaire: Forest Cultures and Kingdoms of the Savannah.*, trans. Scott Bryson. Brussels: Société d'arts primitifs.

1993   "South-East Zaire: Masks of the Luba, Hemba and Tabwa." In *Face of the Spirits: Masks of the Zaire Basin*, eds. Frank Herreman and Constantijn Petridis. Antwerp: Ethnographic Museum, and Washington: Smithsonian Institution, exh. cat.

Nicklin, Keith

1991   *Yoruba: A Celebration of African Art: an exhibition at Horniman Museum and Gardens*. London: Horniman Public Museum and Public Park Trust.

Nicklin, Keith, and Jill Salmons

1984   "Cross River Art Styles." *African Arts* 18 (November): 28-43.

Nooter, Mary (Polly) H.

1984   "The Female Image in Luba Prestige Art." Paper presented at "A Symposium on the History of Art," The Frick Collection and the Institute of Fine Arts of New York University, cosponsors. New York, April 7.

1991   *Luba Art and Polity: Creating Power in a Central African Kingdom*. Ann Arbor, Mich.: University Microfilms.

1993   *Secrecy: African Art that Conceals and Reveals.* New York: The Museum for African Art, exh. cat.

Nooter Roberts, Mary, and Allen F. Roberts.
1996   "Memory: Luba Art and the Making of History." *African Arts* 29:1 (Winter): 22-35, 101-3.

Northern, Tamara
1986   *Expressions of Cameroon Art.* Los Angeles: The Los Angeles County Museum of Natural History, exh. cat.

Novelli, Bruno
1988   *Aspects of Karimojong Ethnosociology.* Verona, Italy: Novastampa di Verona.

Offiong, Daniel A.
1984   "The Functions of the Ekpo Society of the Ibibio of Nigeria." *African Studies Review* 27 (3): 77-92.

Onuwuejeogwu, M. A.
1972-   "The Ikenga—The Cult of Individual Achievements and
73   Advancements." *African Notes* 7 (2): 87-99.

Ottenberg, Simon
1988   "Psychological Aspects of Igbo Art." *African Arts* 21 (2): 72-82.

Pazzaglia, Augusto
1982   *The Karimojong: Some Aspects.* Bologna, Italy: E.M.I.

Peek, Philip M.
1986   "The Isoko Ethos of Ivri." *African Arts* 20 (1): 42-47.

Pemberton, John, III
1975   "Eshu-Elegba. The Yoruba Trickster God." *African Arts* 9 (1): 20-27, 66-70, 90-92.

1995   *Africa: The Art of a Continent.* London: Royal Academy of Arts.

Perrois, Louis
1979   *Arts du Gabon: les arts plastiques du bassin de l'Oquoué.* Arnouville-les-Gonesse: Arts d'Afrique noire.

1985   *Ancestral Arts of Gabon: From the Collections of the Barbier-Müller Museum.*, trans. by Francine Farr. Geneva: Barbier-Müller Museum.

1986   *Ancestral Art of Gabon from the Collections of the Barbier-Müller Museum.*, trans. Francine Farr. Dallas: Dallas Museum of Art, exh. cat.

1986a   *Les Chefs-D'oeuvre de l'Art Gabonais au Musée des Arts et Traditions de Libreville.* Libreville, Gabon.

1995   *Africa: The Art of a Continent.* ed. Tom Phillips. London: Royal Academy of Arts.

Perrois, Louis, and M. Sierra Delage
1990   *The Art of Equatorial Guinea: The Fang Tribes.* New York: Rizzoli.

Philips, John Edward
1983   "African Smoking and Pipes." *Journal of African History* 24 (3): 303-19.

Phillips, Tom, ed.
1995   *Africa: The Art of a Continent.* London: Royal Academy of Arts, exh. cat.

Pickett, Elliot
1971   "The Animal Horn in African Art." *African Arts* 4 (4): 47-53.

Plass, Margaret
1957   *African Negro Sculpture.* Philadelphia: University of Pennsylvania Museum of Art, exh. cat.

Quarcoopome, Nii Otokunor
1985   *Pendant Plaques.* Los Angeles: Museum of Cultural History, University of California.

1993a   "Agbaa: Dangme Art and the Politics of Secrecy." In *Secrecy: African Art that Conceals and Reveals.* New York: The Museum for African Art, exh. cat.

1993b   *Rituals and Regalia of Power: Art and Polities in Dagne and Ewe Cultures, 1800-Present.* Ph.D. diss., University of California at Los Angeles.

Rasmussen, Susan J.
1992   "Ritual Specialists, Ambiguity and Power in Tuareg Society." *Man* 27 (1): 105-28.

Ravenhill, Philip L.
1994   *The Self and the Other.* Los Angeles: Fowler Museum of Cultural History, University of California at Los Angeles, exh. cat.

Rebora, Carrie
1983   "Iron." In *The Art of Power, The Power of Art: Studies in Benin Iconography,* ed. Arnold Rubin and Paula Ben-Amos. Los Angeles: Museum of Cultural History, University of California.

Reefe, Thomas Q.
1981   *The Rainbow and the Kings: a History of the Luba Empire to 1891.* Berkeley: University of California Press.

Richards, J. V. Olufemi
1974   "The Sande Mask." *African Art* 7 (2): 48-51

Robert, Andrew, ed.
1968   *Tanzania before 1900.* Nairobi: The Historical Association of Tanzania.

Roberts, Allen
1986   "Les arts du corps chez les Tabwa." *Arts d'Afrique noire* 59 (Autumn): 15-29.

Roberts, Allen, and Mary Nooter Roberts
1995   *Animals in African Art: From the Familiar to the Fantastic.* New York: Museum for African Art, exh. cat.

Ross, Doran H.

1982 "The Verbal Art of Akan Linguist Staffs." *African Arts* 16 (1): 56-66.

1984 "The Art of Osei Bonsu." *African Arts* 17 (2).

Roy, Christopher D.

1987 "The Spread of Mask Styles in the Black Volta Basin." *African Arts* 20 (4): 40-46, 89.

1987 *Art of the Upper Volta Rivers.* Meudon, France: Alain et Françoise Chaffin.

1992 *Art and Life in Africa: Selections from the Stanley Collection.* Iowa City: University of Iowa Museum of Art, exh. cat.

Rubin, Arnold, ed.

1988 *Marks of Civilization: Artistic Transformations of the Human Body.* Los Angeles: Museum of Cultural History, University of California.

Schaefer, Stacy

1983 "Benin Commemorative Heads." In *The Art of Power, the Power of Art: Studies in Benin Iconography,* ed. Paula Ben-Amos and Arnold Rubin. Los Angeles: Museum of Cultural History, University of California, Monograph Series, no. 19: 71-78, exh. cat.

Scheinberg, Alfred L.

1975 *Art of the Ibo, Ibibio, Ogoni.* New York. exh. cat.

Schildkrout, Enid, and Curtis Keim

1990 *African Reflections: Art from Northeastern Zaire.* Seattle: University of Washington Press.

Schopenhauer, Arthur

1983 "The World as Will and Idea." In *Changing Concepts of Art.* pp. 129-40, New York: Haven Publishing Corporation.

Schweinfurth, Georg

1874 *The Heart of Africa.* 2 vols. New York: Harper and Brothers.

Seattle Art Museum

1984 *Praise Poems: The Katherine White Collection.* Seattle, Seattle Art Museum.

Shapiro, Meyer

1994 *Theory and Philosophy of Art: Style, Artist, and Society.* New York: George Braziller.

Sieber, Roy, and Roslyn A. Walker

1987 *African Art in the Cycle of Life.* Washington, D.C.: National Museum of African Art, exh. cat.

1990 "Fierce and Ugly." In *Art As a Means of Communication in Preliterate Societies,* ed. Dan Eban. pp. 343-53. Jerusalem: The Israel Museum.

Siroto, Leon

1973 "Witchcraft Belief in the Explanation of Traditional African Iconography." In *The Visual Arts: Plastic and Graphic,* ed. Justine M. Cordwell. pp. 241-91. The Hague: Mouton Publishers.

1976 *African Spirit Images and Identities.* New York: Pace Gallery.

Slavin, Kenneth, and Julie Slavin

1973 *The Tuareg.* London: Gentry Books.

Spring, Christopher

1993 *African Arms and Armor.* Washington, D.C.: The Smithsonian Institution Press.

Strother, Zoe S.

1993 "Eastern Pende Constructions of Secrecy." In *Secrecy: African Art that Conceals and Reveals.* New York: The Museum for African Art, exh. cat.

1995 In *Treasures from the African Museum, Turvuren.* Turvuren: Royal Museum for Central Africa.

Sweeney, James Johnson

1964 *African Folktales and Sculpture.* Second ed. New York: Pantheon Books.

Tessman, Günter

1913 *Die Pangwe.* Berlin: E. Wasmuth.

Thomas, E. S.

1925 "The African Throwing Knife." *Journal of the Royal Anthropological Institute* 55.

Thompson, Robert F.

1971 *Black Gods and Kings: Yoruba Art at UCLA.* Los Angeles: Museum and Laboratories of Ethnic Arts and Technology, Occasional Papers, no.2.

1972 "Sign of the Divine King: An Essay on Yoruba Bead-Embroidered Crowns with Veil and Bird Decoration." In *African Art and Leadership,* ed. Douglas Fraser and Herbert Cole. Madison: University of Wisconsin Press.

1973 "Yoruba Artistic Criticism." In *The Traditional Artist in African Societies,* ed. W. D'Azevedo. pp. 18-47. Bloomington: Indiana University Press.

1974 *African Art in Motion.* Los Angeles: University of California Press.

1975 "Icons of the Mind: Yoruba Herbalism in Atlantic Perspective." *African Arts* 8 (3): 52-59, 89-90.

1981 *Four Moments of the Sun: Kongo Art in Two Worlds.* Washington, D.C.: National Gallery of Art.

1983 *Flash of the Spirit: African & Afro-American Art and Philosophy.* New York: Random House.

1994 "The Three Warriors: Atlantic Altars of Esu, Ogun, and Ososi." In *The Yoruba Artist: New Theoretical Perspectives on African Arts,* ed. Henry J. Drewal, John Pemberton III., and Rowland Abiodun, pp. 225-239. Wahington, D.C.: The Smithsonian Institution Press.

Timmermans, Paul
1966 "Essai de typologie de la sculpture des Bena Luluwa du Kasai." *Africa Tervuren* 12 (1): 17-27.

1967 "Les Lwalwa." *Africa Terverun* 13 (3-4): 73-90.

Torday, Emil
1925 *On the Trail of the Bushongo*. London: Seeley, Service, and Co.

Turnbull, Colin M.
1965 *Wayward Servants: The Two Worlds of African Pygmies*. Garden City, N.Y.: Published for the American Museum of Natural History by the Natural History Press.

Uche-Okeke, N. E. O.
1985 "The Relationship of Women to Ikenga." *Ikoro* 6 (2): 21-41.

van Beek, Walter E. A.
1988 "Functions of Sculpture in Dogon Religion." *African Arts* 21 (4): 58-65, 91.

van Geertruyen, Godelieve
1976 "La Fonction de la Sculpture dans une Societé Africaine: Les Baga, Nalu et Landuman (Guinée)." *Africana Gandensia* 1: 63-117.

van Ham, Laurent, and Robert van Dijk
1980 *African Art and Culture of the Upper-Volta*. Rotterdam: R. Schuurman Productions.

Vansina, Jan
1966 *Kingdoms of the Savanna*. London: Regents of the University of Wisconsin.

1968 "Kuba Art and Its Cultural Context." *Africa Forum* 3 (4): 13-27.

1978 *The Children of Woot: A History of the Kuba Peoples*. Madison, Wisc.: University of Wisconsin.

1982 "The Kuba Kingdom (Zaire)." In *Kings of Africa: Art and Authority in Central Africa*, ed. Erna Beumers and Hans-Joachim Koloss. Utrecht, Netherlands: Foundation Kings of Africa, exh. cat.

Visona, Monica Blackmun
1984 *Art and Authority Among the Akye of the Ivory Coast*. Santa Barbara: University of California.

1990 "Portraiture among the Lagoon Peoples of Côte d'Ivoire." *African Arts* 23 (4): 54-61.

Vogel, Susan M.
1977 *Baule Art as an Expression of World View*. Ann Arbor: University Microfilms.

Vogel, Susan M., ed.
1981 *For Spirits and Kings: African Art from the Paul and Ruth Tishman Collection*. New York: The Metropolitan Museum of Art, exh. cat.

Vogel, Susan M., and Francine N'Diaye
1985 *African Masterpieces from the Musée de l'Homme*. New York: Center for African Art, exh. cat.

Volavka, Zdenka
1972 "Nkisi Figures of the Lower Kongo." *African Arts* 5 (2): 52-59.

1977 "Voania Muba: Contributions to the History of Central African Pottery." *African Art* 10 (2): 59-66.

Wachsmann, Klaus
1964 "Human Migration and African Harps." *Journal of International Folk Music* 16: 84-88.

Wardwell, Allen
1986 *African Sculpture from the University Museum, University of Pennsylvania*. Philadelphia: Philadelphia Museum of Art.

Washington, D.C.
1993 National Museum of African Art. *Astonishment and Power*. Washington, D.C.: The Smithsonian Institution Press.

1994 National Museum of African Art. *Beaded Splendor*. Washington, D.C.: The Smithsonian Institution Press.

Webb, Glenn
1985 "Title Societies and Personhood Attainment among the Awka Igbo." *West African Journal of Archaeology* 15: 103-132.

Wescott, Joan
1962 "The Sculpture and Myths of Eshu-Elegba, the Yoruba Trickster." *Africa* 32 (4): 336-54.

Westerdijk, Peter
1988 *The African Throwing Knife*. Utrecht: OMI, University of Utrecht.

Williams, Denis
1974 *Icon and Image: A Study of Sacred and Secular Forms In African Classical Art*. New York: New York University Press.

Wilson, J.G.
1973 "Karamajong." *Uganda Journal* 37: 81-93.

Witte, Hans
1984 *Ifa and Esu: Iconography of Order and Disorder*. Soest Holland: Kunsthandel Luttik.

Wittmer, Marceline Keeling
1976 *Bamum Village Masks*. Ph.D. diss., Bloomington: Indiana University.

Wolff, Norma
1982 "Egungun Costuming in Abeokuta." *African Arts* 15 (3): 66-70, 91.

Zahan, Dominique
1980 *Antilopes du Soleil; Arts et Rites Agraires D'Afrique Noire*. Vienna: Edition A. Schendl.

1974 "The Bambara." *Iconography of Religions* 8 (2).

INDEX

Photo Credits

All works of art in the exhibition were photographed by Dirk Bakker, Director of Photography, except for the Male Power Figure on the cover and on page 49, which were photographed by Robert Hensleigh, Associate Director. All other photographs were supplied by Nii Quarcoopome except the following: page 8, fig. 1 photographed by Fred T. Smith, Kent State University, and page 20, photographed by Eliot Elisofon in 1970 (Eliot Elisofon Photographic Archives, National Museum of African Art, Smithsonian Institution, Washington, D.C.)